Christmas Card Theology

BOOKS BY JAMES D. QUIGGLE

DOCTRINAL SERIES

Biblical History
Adam and Eve, a Biography and Theology
Angelology, a True History of Angels

Essays
Biblical Essays
Biblical Essays II
Biblical Essays III
Biblical Essays IV

Marriage and Family
Marriage and Family: A Biblical Perspective
Biblical Homosexuality
A Biblical Response to Same-gender Marriage

Doctrinal and Practical Christianity
First Steps, Becoming a Follower of Jesus Christ
A Christian Catechism (with Christopher McCuin)
Why and How to do Bible Study
Thirty-Six Essentials of the Christian Faith
The Literal Hermeneutic, Explained and Illustrated
The Old Ten In the New Covenant
Christian Living and Doctrine
Spiritual Gifts
Why Christians Should Not Tithe

Dispensational Theology
A Primer On Dispensationalism
Understanding Dispensational Theology
Covenants and Dispensations in the Scripture
Dispensational Soteriology
Dispensational Eschatology, An Explanation and Defense of the Doctrine
Rapture: A Bible Study on the Rapture of the New Testament Church
Antichrist, His Genealogy, Kingdom, and Religion

God and Man

God's Choices, Doctrines of Foreordination, Election, Predestination
God Became Incarnate
Life, Death, Eternity
Did Jesus Go To Hell?

Small Group Bible Studies
Elementary Bible Principles (with Linda M. Quiggle)
Counted Worthy (with Linda M. Quiggle)

COMMENTARY SERIES

The Old Testament
A Private Commentary on the Bible: Judges
A Private Commentary on the Book of Ruth
A Private Commentary on the Bible: Esther
A Private Commentary on the Bible: Song of Solomon
A Private Commentary on the Bible: Daniel
A Private Commentary on the Bible: Jonah
A Private Commentary on the Bible: Habakkuk
A Private Commentary on the Bible: Haggai

The New Testament
James Quiggle Translation New Testament (JQTNT)

The Gospels and Acts
A Private Commentary on the Bible: Matthew's Gospel
A Private Commentary on the Bible: Mark's Gospel
A Private Commentary on the Bible: Luke 1–12
A Private Commentary on the Bible: Luke 13–24
A Private Commentary on the Bible: John 1–12
A Private Commentary on the Bible: John 13–21
A Private Commentary on the Bible: Acts 1–14
A Private Commentary on the Bible: Acts 15–28

Other Works On the Gospels
Four Voices, One Testimony (a Gospel Harmony)
Jesus Said "I Am"
The Parables and Miracles of Jesus Christ
The Passion and Resurrection of Jesus the Christ
The Christmas Story, As Told By God

Christmas Card Theology and the Bible (With David Hollingsworth)

Pauline Letters

A Private Commentary on the Bible: Galatians
A Private Commentary on the Bible: Ephesians
A Private Commentary on the Bible: Philippians
A Private Commentary on the Bible: Colossians
A Private Commentary on the Bible: Thessalonians
A Private Commentary on the Bible: Pastoral Letters
A Private Commentary on the Bible: Philemon

General Letters

A Private Commentary on the Book of Hebrews
A Private Commentary on the Bible: James
A Private Commentary on the Bible: 1 Peter
A Private Commentary on the Bible: 2 Peter
A Private Commentary on the Bible: John's Epistles
A Private Commentary on the Bible: Jude

Revelation

A Private Commentary on the Bible: Revelation 1–7
A Private Commentary on the Bible: Revelation 8–16
A Private Commentary on the Bible: Revelation 17–22

REFERENCE SERIES

James Quiggle Translation New Testament (JQT)
Dictionary of Doctrinal Words
Old and New Testament Chronology (With David Hollingsworth)
(Also in individual volumes: Old Testament Chronology; New Testament Chronology)

TRACTS

A Human Person: Is the Unborn Life a Person?
Biblical Marriage
How Can I Know I am A Christian?
Now That I am A Christian
Thirty-Six Essentials of the Christian Faith
What is a Pastor? / Why is My Pastor Eating the Sheep?
Principles and Precepts of the Literal Hermeneutic

(All tracts are in digital format and cost $0.99)

Formats
Print, Digital, Epub, PDF. Search "James D. Quiggle" or book title.

Christmas Card Theology and the Bible

James D. Quiggle

With David R. Hollingsworth

Copyright page

Christmas Card Theology and the Bible

Copyright 2024, James D. Quiggle

ISBN: 979-8-9871044-6-0

Permissions: Any random selection of 10–15 questions out of the total 57 questions may be used during any annual Christmas season by local church pastors or Bible class teachers during one regular service or Bible class during any annual Christmas season. Each annual Christmas season the same 10–15 questions or a different random selection of 10–15 questions may be used. The answers may be used, but not the explanations. If you want your church members to know the explanations recommend the book. Individuals, parachurch organizations, missionaries, etc., teaching Scripture or leading worship or praise services may use this book as described above. If you want those to whom you are ministering to know the explanations recommend the book.

New Testament scriptures are from *James Quiggle Translation New Testament* (JQTNT), copyright 2023, James D. Quiggle.

Old Testament scriptures not otherwise marked are the author's translation.

Old Testament scriptures marked LXX are from *The Septuagint with Apocrypha: English*, by Sir Lancelot C. L. Brenton. Public Domain.

The original questions and answers that are the basis for this book are from David R. Hollingsworth, used by permission of his widow and executor of his estate, Kathleen Hollingsworth. All editing, modifications, deletions, or additions to the original questions and answers are solely the responsibility of James D. Quiggle.

This print edition contains the same material as the digital editions.

Cover. Julius Garibaldi Melchers, *The Nativity*, ca. 1891.

Table of Contents

Introduction 13
A Challenge 17
The Fifty-Seven Questions 19
The 57 Questions With Answers and Explanations 23
Sources and Resources 173

Introduction

The origin of the Christmas Card Theology Quiz is lost to time. Greeting cards have a long history, stretching back to ancient Egypt. In the 1400s handmade greeting cards were being exchanged in Europe, and not long afterward printed. The first American greeting card company was founded in 1903.

The first Christmas card dates to 1843, in England. In 1915 the Hallmark company made its first Christmas cards. Most likely it was not too long before some pastor saw an opportunity to preach against a secularized Christmas. The Christmas Card Theology Quiz probably had a long development, handed down from pastor to pastor.

Perhaps the first Christmas Card Theology Quiz was developed after Hollywood began making Christmas movies (1898); or perhaps after television began broadcasting Christmas Specials (1957). The date and place of the first Quiz is unknown. Regardless of when, there is a definite Christmas theology taught by Christmas cards, movies, and television, which has little to do with the Bible's Christmas story.

I first learned of the Christmas Card Theology Quiz in Christmas 1977, at First Baptist Church, Cambria California, under the leadership of Pastor David R. Hollingsworth. I listened to him read fourteen questions in 1977, 1978, and 1979—the same fourteen questions each time—and then read them again with the answers. I failed the quiz each year.

I was twenty-five years of age in 1977, having been saved three years before, May 19, 1974. During those twenty-two years I had zero contact with genuine Christianity, and the theology subtly taught by Christmas card theology was difficult to overcome. I am now almost 72. I have learned the Christmas story as taught by God in the Scripture. Thus this book, with prayer for those held captive by Christmas card theology.

My military career moved me away from Cambria before Christmas 1980. Pastor Dave and I kept in touch via "snail mail" (no internet in those days, no cell phones). Not long after I moved I asked him for a copy of his Annual Christmas Card Theology Quiz, which was provided. I began using his quiz annually in the Bible classes I taught in several churches in the USA and Germany (again, a military career). When he gave me a copy of the quiz, he confessed he had gotten it from his pastor, and he from his pastor, etc. A long line of pastors is responsible for the first versions of the Quiz, passed down from spiritual father to spiritual son.

When I began to engage on social media I posted the quiz annually, questions first, and then answers in a later post. I still use the original fourteen questions; no one has ever answered all fourteen questions correctly.

These are the original fourteen questions I received from Pastor Hollingsworth about 1980–81.

1. What O.T. prophet foretold the virgin birth?
2. Fill in the blanks properly: "For unto us a _____ is born, unto us a _____ is given."
3. Mary and Jesus are the true Madonna and Child—yes or no?
4. Did the angel Gabriel appear first to Mary or Joseph?
5. Did Mary understand who her son was?
6. What did the angels sing to the shepherds?
7. Did Christ come to bring peace to the world—yes or no?
8. Did the Magi follow the star from the east—yes or no?
9. How many wise men were there?
10. Who were the first evangelists to proclaim Messiah's birth?
11. Did the wise men visit Jesus in a manger?
12. Did the baby Jesus have a halo?
13. Jesus' birth is called the immaculate conception?
14. How many gifts did the Magi bring?

Pastor Hollingsworth's notes indicate he began adding to the original fourteen in 1987. He kept track of what questions he used in what year. By Christmas 2005 the number of questions had increased to fifty-seven.

Pastor Hollingsworth died May 2012. By that time I was a Christian author. Pastor Hollingsworth's avocation over his forty years of pastoral ministry was biblical chronology. Before his death he gave me permission to edit and publish his biblical chronology manuscript. *New Testament Chronology* was published in 2014, *Old Testament Chronology* in 2015, and also in 2015 I published a one volume edition,

Old and New Testament Chronology. His is a rich legacy, and I owe him much.

The year is now January 2024. Pastor Hollingsworth's widow has told me she found a copy of the Christmas Card Theology Quiz in Pastor's Hollingsworth files, with fifty-seven questions. I have been given permission by Mrs. Hollingsworth to develop and publish this book. I have lightly edited Pastor Hollingsworth's original questions and answers, replaced one question (an attempt at humor with a play on the words "pilot" and "Pilate") with one of my own, deleted one, and added one.

The work is arranged in this manner. The first chapter is the fifty-seven questions without answers.

The second chapter is each of the fifty-seven questions, one by one, with answer and explanation.

This is the format for the answers.

Christmas Card Theology teaches …. What does the Scripture say?

Answer:

Explanation:

The answers are from Pastor Hollingsworth, lightly edited here and there by me. The "Christmas Card Theology teaches …" and the explanations for each question are wholly mine.

Sources, Resources, And Translations

Most sources and resources used in the explanations are in the final chapter. Some resources are unnamed, because they are long ago studies frequently used in teaching and writing ministries, and thereby forever incorporated into memory.

Old Testament translations are from one of two sources.

The Septuagint, identified as LXX, a Greek translation of the Hebrew Old Testament Scripture dated to 285–246 BC.

The author's translation, using the Westminster Leningrad Codex at biblehub.com/interlinear.

Occasionally the LXX text does not read the same as extant Hebrew texts. Hence the variation in translation sources.

All New Testament translations are from the *James Quiggle Translation New Testament*. That brings up the translation of the Greek word *ággelos*.

In his Quiz questions, Paster Hollingsworth used the word "angel," because his congregation had been trained by English Bible versions, as you have been trained, to think of the created spirit beings as "angels."

In the JQTNT, *ággelos* is translated "messenger." The word "angel" is *ággelos* transliterated, not translated. The Greek word means "messenger," and that is the translation used in the JQTNT.

Sometimes in the Scripture *ággelos* is a human messenger and sometimes *ággelos* is one of God's spirit being messengers. The same is true for the Hebrew word *ma'lāk*, which means "messenger," but in almost every English version is deliberately mistranslated as "angel." The context of a Scripture using *ággelos* readily identifies the kind of *ággelos* in view.

In the JQTNT the name Mariám is transliterated as Mariam, not Mary. In the questions Pastor Hollingsworth's "Mary" has been retained. In the explanations I use Mariam.

For other questions about the JQTNT, consult the Preface and the Translation Notes in that work.

A Challenge

First answer the questions without looking at the answers. Then, read the answers and explanations. Take your time; Christmas comes but once a year; become prepared to respond to Christmas card theology.

The Fifty-Seven Questions

Answer the questions before reading the next chapter. You might be surprised at the influence Christmas card theology has in your life.

1. What Scripture verse goes back farther than any other with regard to Christ's "beginnings?"

2. What Old Testament prophet foretold the virgin birth of the God-man.

3. When God spoke through the prophet Isaiah to King Ahaz, the king was given a prophetic sign: "behold, a virgin shall conceive in the womb, and shall bring forth a son, and thou shalt call his name _____."

4. Fill in the blanks from Isaiah 9:6, "For a _____ is born to us, and a _____ is given to us."

5. Through the prophet Isaiah, God said the name of the virgin-born son would be composed of four compound titles. What are they?

6. What prophet foretold the name of the village where Jesus would be born?

7. What scripture gives the specific location in Bethlehem where Jesus was born, that is, which barn?

8. How many times did an angel or angels appear in connection with the overall Christman story?

9. What were the names of the angels who appeared to Zacharias? To Mary? To Joseph?

10. Did an angel appear first to Joseph or to Mary?

11. Did the angel appear to Joseph before or after Mary was expecting the baby Jesus?

12. When Joseph knew Mary was pregnant, what did he initially plan to do?

13. Was Jesus birth a miracle?

14. Is the birth of Jesus called the immaculate conception?

15. Mary and Jesus are the true Madonna and Child—yes or no?

16. Was Jesus born in Galilee, Samaria, or Judea?

17. By what means of conveyance (mode of transportation) did Joseph and Mary travel to Bethlehem for Jesus' Birth?

18. Did Mary ride a donkey from Nazareth to Bethlehem?

19. Why was Mary's baby to be named Jesus, according to the angel?

20. Considering that Joseph and Mary lived in Nazareth, why did Jesus come to be born in Bethlehem?

21. What was the reason, or reasons, Joseph and Mary left Nazareth and went to Bethlehem?

22. Of what Hebrew tribe were Joseph and Mary?

23. Did Joseph legally wed Mary before or after the birth of Jesus?

24. When was the name "Jesus" first given to the child to be born of Mary?

25. When was the name "Jesus" given a second time to the child to be born of Mary?

26. When did Mary's first-born child actually receive his name legally and officially?

27. What month and year was Jesus born?

28. Why is it reasonable to assume Jesus was not born in December?

29. Did someone (an innkeeper?) provide or send Joseph and Mary to a stable?

30. Did Mary know exactly whom her son, Jesus, was?

31. Did Joseph know exactly whom his son, Jesus, was?

32. Did Jesus come to bring peace into the world?

33. Which gospel does not tell the Christmas story?

34. Was the announcement to the shepherds by one angel or many angels?

35. What did the angels sing to the shepherds?

36. Where did the shepherds find the newly-born Jesus?

37. How old was Jesus when the shepherds came to visit him?

38. Did the shepherds know exactly that Jesus was both Savior and Messiah?

39. Did the baby Jesus have a halo?

40. Who were the first recorded human witnesses for Christ?

41. Was shepherding considered a very noble profession?

42. What was Jesus' first recorded journey?

43. Who recognized Jesus as Messiah, and blessed him, during Jesus' first recorded journey?

44. Who is the second recorded human witness for Christ?

45. Where did Jesus and his family live immediately after he was presented in Jerusalem?

46. Of the wise men who visited Jesus and his family, how many were there, and what were their names?

47. Were the wise men kings, as in the carol, "We Three Kings of Orient are?"

48. Where were the Magi from?

49. Did the wise men follow the star from the east?

50. When Herod heard about Jesus, was he the only one troubled by the news?

51. Did the wise men visit Jesus in the stable?

52. How old was Jesus when the wise men saw him?

53. Did Jesus' ancestors include a prostitute, an adulteress, a woman who committed incest, and a former pagan gentile?

54. What words of Joseph are recorded in the Christmas story?

55. Were the angels chubby little cherubs?

56 Did Jesus' family celebrate his birthday as we do today?

57. Were sheep, cattle, a donkey, kings, angels, shepherds, and a little drummer boy present in the stable after Jesus was born?

The 57 Questions With Answers and Explanations

1. What Scripture verse goes back farther than any other with regard to Christ's "beginnings?"

Christmas Card Theology teaches Christ's beginning was in a stable in Bethlehem. What does the Scripture say?

Answer: John 1:1–2 says, "In the beginning was the Word and the Word was with God and God was the Word. He was in the beginning with God."

Explanation: The Christ is an office of God the Son, Psalm 2:2, 7, that began with the union of God the Son with Jesus of Nazareth, an act known as the incarnation. The person formed in the incarnation is the Christ, the God-man, the Son of God, a person with one personality, that of God the Son, informed by his two natures, genuine deity and genuine human. The Christ is God the Son incarnate with Jesus of Nazareth, who is the God-man, the Son of God.

Are we justified in saying the Scripture presents Jesus the Christ as the God-man? Yes.

> Colossians 2:9, "For in him [Christ, 2:6, 8] dwells all the fullness of the deity in bodily form."

> Hebrews 1:3, "who [1:1, the Son] being the shining of his [1:1, God] glory and his [1:1, God] exact essence."

God the Son is increate, Exodus 3:14, and therefore does not have a beginning. He was before the beginning; he created the beginning, Genesis 1:1; he was present "in the beginning," John 1:1–2. He was present in the beginning because he is increate, Exodus 3:14, "I am he who exists," having life-in-himself, John 5:26.

Jesus of Nazareth is a genuine human being whose beginning was Luke 1:35, 38.

> Luke 1:35, "And responding the messenger said to her, 'The Holy Spirit will come upon you, and the power of Most High will rest upon you. Therefore also the holy begotten

will be called, 'Son of God.'"

Luke 1:38, "Then Mariam said, 'See the handmaid of the Lord. May it be to me according to your word.' And the messenger departed from her."

The Christ has a dual presence in the universe: the increate eternal limitless God; the finite, limited human being conceived in Mariam. The genuine humanity of the Christ is as important as his genuine deity. He must be mortal to suffer the penalty for sin, death. He must be deity to give his death limitless merit. The union of genuine deity with genuine humanity formed the God-man.

In relation to the incarnate person Jesus the Christ, the Scripture verse that goes back farther than any other is Psalm 2:7 (LXX), "declaring the ordinance of the Lord: the Lord said to me, 'Thou [2:2, the anointed, aka: Messiah; aka: Christ] art my Son, to-day have I begotten thee.'"

2. What Old Testament prophet foretold the virgin birth of the God-man.

Christmas Card Theology downplays the prophetic aspects of the Christ's birth, and although it mentions a virgin birth, it never speaks of the virgin conception. What does the Scripture say?

Answer: the prophet Isaiah foretold the virgin conception and virgin birth of the God-man.

Isaiah 7:14 (LXX), "Therefore the Lord himself shall give you a sign; behold, a virgin shall conceive in the womb, and shall bring forth a son, and thou shalt call his name Emmanuel."

Explanation: To speak of only the virgin birth ignores the fact the prophecy speaks of conception in a virgin and birth by a virgin. What is in view concerning the Christ is a supra-naturally induced conception without physical, sexual intercourse, and therefore continuing virginity from conception through the birth.

How do we know Isaiah 7:14 is about the conception and birth of the God-man, Jesus the Christ? Because a messenger from God said so in the inspired, inerrant Word of God.

Matthew 1:20–22, "… behold, a messenger of the Lord in a dream appeared to Joseph, saying, 'Joseph, son of David, do not fear to receive Mariam as your wife, for that conceived in her is from the Holy Spirit. 21 She will bear a son, and you will call his name Jesus; for he will save his people from their sins.' 22 So all this was done that may be fulfilled that having been spoken by the Lord through the prophet, saying: 23 'Behold, the virgin shall be with child, and bear a son, and they shall call his name Immanuel,' which is translated, 'God with us.'"

Jesus the Christ was born ca. 5 BC. About 740 BC, Isaiah says that YHWH [the meaning of the all caps LORD] gave the prophecy Isaiah 7:10–14. YHWH Elohim [LORD God] told King Ahaz to "Ask for a sign," that he might know the prophecy in 7:7–9 would come to pass. Ahaz would not ask, so YHWH gave him a sign, Isaiah 7:14, "a virgin shall conceive in the womb, and shall bring forth a son," and before that child knew the difference between right and wrong, the King of Syria and the

King of Samaria would die.

Obviously, in 740 BC a specific virgin woman conceiving a child and giving birth as a sign to King Ahaz was not Mariam (Mary) of Nazareth, who was born about 20 BC. Moreover, the word translated "virgin" is the Hebrew ʿalmâ, which means "a young woman, one of whose characteristics is virginity" (from Harris, *Theological Wordbook of the Old Testament*, word number 1630b.) The word ʿalmâ refers to an unmarried female of marriageable age (menstruation had begun but no sexual intercourse had occurred).

The ancient Greek translation of the Hebrew Old Testament, the Septuagint (aka: LXX), used the Greek word *parthénos*, as did the messenger in Matthew 1:23, which does mean "virgin." That is how the Hebrews understood ʿalmâ in Isaiah 7:14. A virgin woman would conceive and give birth.

Therefore, we are assured by those who translated the Hebrew scriptures into Greek (the LXX), that the prophecy in Isaiah 7:14 means a virgin conceiving and giving birth. No other details are given, because the details in 740 BC were not the same as in 5 BC. Only the Holy Spirit knew all the details and he did not tell Isaiah, or those listening, or those later reading the prophecy during Old Testament times.

Within the historical context in which the prophecy was given, King Ahaz and those hearing, and later reading, the Isaiah scripture passage, including Isaiah, during Old Testament times, would have thought of a virgin woman marrying and conceiving a child through the natural processes of conception and birth. The ʿalmâ might have been a virgin Isaiah would marry. That is the within context, historical interpretation that Isaiah and others understood.

About 740 years after the Isaiah 7:14 prophecy was given, that specific prophecy was by the Holy Spirit applied to Mariam of Nazareth, through the inspired writer Matthew. The Holy Spirit knew in 740 BC what no one during Old Testament times could know: a woman of marriageable age who was a virgin would conceive a child by supra-natural means. Luke 1:31–38, confirms this interpretation.

By the processes of divine inspiration, Matthew gained from the Holy Spirit an application of Isaiah 7:14 that specifically applied to Mariam of Nazareth, no one else, and fully agrees with Luke 1:35, "The Holy Spirit will come upon you [Mariam], and the power of Most High will rest upon you. Therefore also the holy begotten will be called, 'Son of God.'"

That particular inspired application of Isaiah 7:14—that it applied to Mariam of Nazareth in such a way that it applied to no one else in that way—in the particular sense that Mariam was virgin but pregnant, and continued to be sexually a virgin through the birth, was communicated through one of God's messengers to Joseph. The messenger assured Joseph that Mariam's pregnancy was not natural—not by sexual intercourse—but by supra-natural means, "for that conceived in her is from the Holy Spirit."

We can go a little further in the Scripture to validate the virgin conception and birth. (In chronological order).

Luke 1:34–35, "Then said Mariam to the messenger, 'How will this be, since I know not a man [sexually]?' 35 And responding the messenger said to her, 'The Holy Spirit will come upon you, and the power of Most High will rest upon you.'"

Matthew 1:24–25, "Then Joseph, being aroused from sleep, did as the messenger of the Lord commanded him and took to him his wife, 25 and did not know her [sexually] until she had brought forth her firstborn son. And he called his name Jesus."

The only way to deny the virgin conception and virgin birth of Jesus the Christ in Mariam of Nazareth is to deny the authenticity, accuracy, and credibility of the inspired inerrant Word of God.

3. When God spoke through the prophet Isaiah to King Ahaz, the king was given a prophetic sign: "behold, a virgin shall conceive in the womb, and shall bring forth a son, and thou shalt call his name _____."

>Christmas Card Theology seldom states the name given by prophecy in Isaiah, as it is a declaration of an uncomfortable truth, that prophecy given by God genuinely announces specific future events. What does the Scripture say?
>
>Answer: Immanuel, Isaiah 7:14.
>
>Explanation: In Isaiah 7:14, a human being was to be born who would be known as "God with us," the literal translation of the Hebrew `immānûēl*. (The suffix *ēl* is one of three Hebrews words for "God.") In Matthew 1:23, the Holy Spirit, through the messenger's announcement to Joseph, applies that name to Jesus, using the Greek equivalent, *emmanouḗl*, of the Hebrew `immānûēl*.
>
>Within the historical context of the Isaiah prophecy, YHWH gave King Ahaz assurance that YHWH would be with Israel (`immānûēl*) to defeat Israel's enemies, at that time Syria and Samaria, Isaiah 7:1. (Note: 200 years earlier, following the death of Solomon, the nation Israel had divided into two kingdoms: southern Judah; northern Israel-Samaria.)
>
>The name Immanuel is given three times: Isaiah 7:14; 8:8; Matthew 1:23. In the Isaiah 7:14 passage the name of the child to be born indicates "God [is] with us" in that time of trouble.
>
>In Matthew 1:23 the messenger quotes Isaiah 7:14 to tell Joseph that Mariam's conceived but as yet unborn child is (not will be, but is from conception forward) "God with us." The messenger had just told Joseph, 1:21, to "call his name Jesus" which translated is "Savior." The truth is evident: Jesus will be the Savior just because he will be "God with us." Here is the incarnation and its reason in two verses. God chose to become one with us—in union with a member of the human race—as the means to save sinful human beings.
>
>Therefore, the names given to Mariam's son. "Jesus," Matthew 1:21, "he will save his people from their sins," and "Immanuel,"

Isaiah 7:14; Matthew 1:23, "God with us," tell us who he was: "God with us Savior."

When we look at the entire testimony of Scripture, in the four gospels and the New Testament letters, e.g., Colossians 2:9, "in him [Christ] dwells all the fullness of the deity in bodily form," the name "Immanuel" tells us who Mariam's son was: God incarnate. His name "Jesus" tells us why he came: to save his people from their sins. His names and titles tell us the works he came to accomplish: the God-man who came to be Revealer of God, Redeemer of sinners, and King of his people. Jesus the Christ is Prophet, Priest, and King.

"As a king sends his son, who is also a king, so sent God Christ; as God he sent him; as to men he sent him; as a Savior he sent him" [*Letter of Mathetes to Diognetus*, circa AD 130, by an unknown "disciple of the Apostles."]

God-with-us hearkens back to man's creation. Man was created to be "with God." Genesis 1:26 (LXX), "And God said, Let us make man according to our image and likeness." God created humankind for fellowship with himself. Through his sin the first human being, Adam, caused great injury to that fellowship. God restored Adam and the Woman to fellowship with himself, but that fellowship could never be as unhindered, as freely given and received, as it had been when Adam and Eve were sinless.

After Adam's sin, God never again walked with man as he had in the Garden, because sin had turned humankind away from the righteous state of "with God." To correct that problem God became incarnate in a man so that he could be "with us." In Jesus Christ the image and likeness of humankind was restored to its pristine state. By Jesus Christ the state of "with God" was restored when the incarnation made God the Son to be the God-man, which is to say, "God with us."

Through saving faith in Jesus Christ those redeemed by that faith from the penalty of sin are made to be with God.

4. Fill in the blanks from Isaiah 9:6, "For a _____ is born to us, and a _____ is given to us."

Christmas Card Theology teaches a baby was born, but ignores the prophecy and its meaning. What does the Scripture say?

Answer: "For a child is born to us, and a son is given to us."

Explanation: Isaiah 9:6 is really not about Christmas, but the coming Messiah-King. We today tend to think of the Messiah-Christ as Redeemer and King, but in the Old Testament the Holy Spirit presented two distinct lines of messianic prophecy, a coming Messiah-King and a coming Messiah-Redeemer. Yes, you and I know that is the same person, but the reason we know is we have the New Testament revelation that told us Messiah-Redeemer and Messiah-King are the same person.

The Holy Spirit never confuses or conflates those two distinct lines of prophecy in Old Testament Scripture. The reason is the Holy Spirit knew the Messiah would have two advents, the first as Redeemer, the second as King.

Only the briefest of outlines may be given here. The Messiah-King prophecy begins at Genesis 49:10, and is expanded at 2 Samuel 7:13, 16. Psalm 2 is David's commentary on the 2 Samuel 7:13, 16 prophecy of the coming king that was given to him by the prophet Nathan. Isaiah 9:6 is part of the continuing line of Messiah-King prophecy, as is Matthew's genealogy and Luke 1:17, 32.

The Messiah-Redeemer line of prophecy begins at Genesis 12:3, as we discover at Galatians 3:8. Daniel 9:26, "Messiah will be cut-off and have nothing for himself" is part of that prophecy.

(Yes, you know of other scriptures of Messiah-Redeemer, such as Isaiah 53. How do you know Isaiah 53 is about the Messiah-Redeemer? Because the New Testament revelation told you so, compare Acts 8:32–35. The Old Testament peoples did not have the New Testament revelation, and therefore did not connect the Messiah-King prophecies with the Messiah-Redeemer prophecies. Bear in mind the Hebrew *māshîah* is used of the coming Messiah-Christ only in Psalm 2:2, the Messiah-King, and Daniel 9:25, 26, the Messiah-Redeemer.)

In Isaiah 9:6 the emphasis is not on "us" but on the one born and given. He is the Coming One who will sit on David's throne, 2 Samuel 7:13, 16. In New Testament terms, in Isaiah 9:6 the second advent is in view.

The messenger Gabriel announces this coming King to Mariam, Luke 1:32–33, "He will be great, and will be called 'son of Most High.' And the Lord God will give him the throne of David, his father. 33 And he will reign over the house of Jacob to the ages, and of his kingdom there will not be an end."

Jesus the Messiah (Christ) began his active ministry after his baptism by his herald, who was sent to proclaim the Messiah-King who would redeem the nation Israel from their national enemies. That is how Zacharias understood the function of the herald, Luke 1:74, and how Mariam understood her son, Luke 1:51–54. That is why John the Baptist questioned if Jesus was the Messiah he was proclaiming as coming King now arrived, Matthew 11:2–3, because Jesus was healing, not conquering.

That is also how the apostles understood the Messiah, as a king to redeem the nation, not a redeemer of individuals from the penalty of sin. Jesus had begun by proclaiming the kingdom. About two years later he changes his message from Messiah-King to Messiah-Redeemer, Matthew 16:21. Did the apostles understand? No. Matthew 16:22.

Matthew 16:21–22, "From that time Jesus began to show to his disciples that it is necessary for him to go away to Jerusalem, and to suffer many things from the elders and chief priests and scribes, and to be killed, and on the third day to be raised. 22 And having taken him aside, Peter began to rebuke him, saying, 'Far be it from you, master; no, this will never be to you.'"

Peter, taught in the synagogue by the scribes, rejected a Messiah-Redeemer, who must die (and resurrect), because like all others in Israel he was looking for a Messiah-King who must conquer and rule.

A little history will help. Historian Emil Schurer, in his work, *A History of the Jewish People in the Time of Jesus Christ*, Division 2, 2:129–130, had this observation.

"The older Messianic hope virtually moves within the boundary of the then present circumstances of the world, and is nothing else than the hope of a better future for the *nation*. That the nation should be morally purified from all bad elements, that it should exist unmolested and respected in the midst of the Gentile world, whilst its enemies were either destroyed or forced to acknowledge the nation and its God, that it should be governed by a just, wise, and powerful king of the house of David, and that therefore internal justice, peace and happiness would prevail, nay that all natural evils would be abolished and a state of unclouded prosperity would appear—this may be said to have formed the foundation of the future hope among the older prophets."

Isaiah 9:6 is a prophecy of the coming Messiah-King. The focus is on his birth. The Messiah-King will be born to human parents, as Isaiah 9:6 implies, "unto us" he is born, "unto us" he is given. True to the prophecy, the Messiah-King was born of Mariam of Nazareth, in Bethlehem, as prophesied in the prophet Micah.

The nation rejected the deliverance promised by the King. That rejection was known by the sovereign God, and the time of the King is right where it always was on God's calendar, after the second advent. Isaiah 9:6 prophesies the birth, but its focus is on the King of the second advent.

5. Through the prophet Isaiah, God said the name of the virgin-born son would be composed of four compound titles. What are they?

> Christmas card theology tends to ignore all but one of the titles of the Christ, Prince of Peace. What does the Scripture say?
>
> Answer: Wonderful Counselor; Mighty God; Everlasting Father; Prince of Peace.
>
> Explanation: Isaiah 9:6, "For a child is born unto us, a son is given unto us. And the government will be upon his shoulder, and his name will be called wonderful counselor, mighty God, everlasting Father, prince of peace."
>
> Regardless of what the Jews thought of Isaiah 9:6, Christians have accepted these four titles as describing Jesus the Christ. However, the context is important. These titles become effective at the second advent, when the child born unto us sits on the throne of David, Isaiah 9:7, agreeable to the prophecy of 2 Samuel 7:13, 16, and the king and his kingdom described in Psalm 2, and the announcement in Luke 1:32–33.
>
> Jesus announced the Davidic-Messianic kingdom in the first part of his earthly ministry, Matthew 3:2; Mark 1:15. The Jews rejected Jesus as their Messiah-King, and he redirected his ministry to his function as Messiah-Redeemer, see Matthw 16:21–27; Mark 8:31–38; Luke 9:22–26. The rejection of the Kingdom was, of course, known to the sovereign God, and the kingdom was and is where it always was on God's prophetic calendar, after the second advent.
>
> Did Jesus come as the Prince of Peace to the world in his first advent, as Christmas card theology proclaims? Jesus answered that question at Matthew 10:34–35, "Think not that I came to bring peace to the earth. I came not to bring peace, but a sword. 35 For I came to incite a man against his father; and a daughter against her mother; and a daughter-in-law against her mother-in-law; 36 and the man's enemies his household."
>
> However, Jesus Christ does bring peace to those he saves from the penalty due sin, which penalty is alienation from God during this mortal life, Romans 8:7–8, and endless punishment in the life to come, Revelation 20:11–15. Jesus reconciles the sinner

to God, bringing peace between God the now saved sinner. By God's grace through faith the sinner is reconciled to God (saved, Ephesians 2:8, Acts 16:31) and has peace with God.

Jesus Christ gives peace with God to those he has saved, those who have faith in the crucified and risen Jesus Christ as their Savior. Romans 5:1, "Therefore, having been justified by faith, we have peace with God through our Lord Jesus Christ."

The gospel of reconciliation with God through the crucified and risen Savior is the Christmas message.

6. What prophet foretold the name of the village where Jesus would be born?

> Christmas Card Theology seldom mentions the prophets (Isaiah is occasionally the exception), because that would require a belief in all the prophecies concerning Jesus Christ, and belief in an inspired, inerrant Scripture. What does the Scripture say?

Answer: the prophet Micah

Explanation: YHWH gave the prophet Micah this prophecy, as recorded in Micah 5:2 (LXX), "And thou, Bethleem, house of Ephratha, art few in number to be reckoned among the thousands of Juda; yet out of thee shall one come forth to me, to be a ruler of Israel; and his goings forth were from the beginning, even from eternity."

Bethlehem Ephratha was about five miles south of Jerusalem. Micah's prophecy specified Bethlehem Ephratha because at the time the prophecy was given there was another village named Bethlehem in the tribal territory of Zebulon (in the region later known as Galilee).

YHWH God gave the prophet Micah the prophecy ca. 731–700 BC. Jesus was born in Bethlehem ca. 5 BC.

At this point someone may be asking, if BC means "Before Christ," and AD means "in the year of our Lord," then why wasn't Jesus born in 1 BC or 1 AD? The short answer is that in AD 525 the Roman Catholic Church monk assigned to create a new calendar based on the birth of Christ, decided Jesus was born a few months before Herod died in April 754 AUC, i.e., 754 *Anno Urbis Conditae*, 754 years after the city of Rome was founded.

However, centuries later it was discovered Herod died in 750 AUC. By that time every historical event from past to present was arranged according to the monk's BC–AD calendar. Rather than change every historical date, historians adjusted the date of Christ's birth to somewhere between 7–4 BC.

I have defended a 5 BC birth year in my book *God Became Incarnate*.

7. What scripture gives the specific location in Bethlehem where Jesus was born?

> Christmas Card Theology implies Jesus was born in a stable or barn, because it shows the newly born Jesus lying in a feeding trough sometimes surrounded by various animals. What does the Scripture say?
>
> Answer: Micah 4:8, "And you, the Tower of the Flock, the stronghold of the daughter of Zion, to you it will come, to you will come the dominion, the former kingdom of the daughter of Jerusalem."
>
> Explanation: The Tower of the Flock is a tall tower built of stone blocks, set on a rock foundation, with a cave underneath, located about nine-tenths of a mile north of Bethlehem—close enough to be considered (in modern terms) a suburb of Bethlehem. Joseph and Mariam passed the tower on the road between Jerusalem and Bethlehem. Micah 5:2 gave the general location of Jesus' birth, Micah 4:8 stated exactly where Jesus would be born.
>
> In relation to the birth, Micah said, as surely as Babylon will take Judah into captivity and then be judged, so will the Christ be born at the Tower of the Flock (4:8) in Bethlehem-Ephrathah (5:2).
>
> In the Old Testament the tower was near to where Rachel was buried, Genesis 35:19, 21. In Micah's time the cave under the tower had long been used as a barn or stable by local shepherds.
>
> The "manger" in which Jesus was laid was not a feeding trough, but the barn in the cave under the Tower. God's messenger told the shepherds they would find the baby in "the *phátnē*." In Greek, more so than in English, the definite article indicates specific identity. The word *phátnē* [Zodhiates, s. v. 5336] can mean "a feeding trough," or a "stable." A stable, aka: barn, is its true meaning here. Compare Luke 13:15, where a donkey is loosed from its *phátnē* to be lead to water. The word may mean "stall" at Luke 13:15 but it certainly does not mean "feeding trough."

Some ancient writers claim the cave was the barn for the shepherds keeping the sacrificial sheep for the Jerusalem temple. It seems likely that in the days of Joseph and Mariam, the cave under the tower was used during inclement weather and for birthing lambs by shepherds raising sheep for the temple. I think it a safe assumption the shepherds to whom God's messengers appeared knew the prophecies related to their home and work. Certainly they were able to go with haste and find the babe.

Finally, the contrast in Luke 2:7 is not between an inn and a feeding trough, but between an inn and a place large enough to substitute for an inn for at least one little family. Mariam gave birth in the barn in the cave used for keeping animals, located under the Tower of the Flock, just as Micah had prophesied.

The English word "inn" is a mistranslation. The Greek word is *katáluma* [Zodhiates, s. v. 2646] which means "lodging." A *katáluma* in New Testament times could be a guest room in a house, an open area surrounded by a wall with niches in the wall for people and animals, or a large open area where travelers gathered and camped out in the open for the night. Considering many people had come to Bethlehem for the registration, Luke 2:1–3, the lack of room in any kind of *katáluma* was understandable, and providential, as it sent Jospeh and Miriam to the *phátnē* under the Tower of the Flock.

Joseph and Mariam probably knew the main messianic prophecy in the book of Micah 5:2. Mariam may not have attended the local synagogue school when she was a child, but she attended synagogue services every Sabbath. She knew Scripture (see Luke 1:46–55, which is composed of many Old Testament scriptures). So also Joseph, who would have attended synagogue school when he was a child, as well as Sabbath services.

When they found no room in a *katáluma* in Bethlehem—because of the great number of people present for the enrollment—they remembered they had passed the tower on the way into Bethlehem; at that time the Spirit may have brought Micah 4:8 to their remembrance. Regardless, they turned around, walked the 20 minutes or so to the tower (nine-tenths of a mile), and there Mariam gave birth to Jesus, according to Micah's prophecies, at Bethlehem-Ephrathah, at the Tower of the Flock. She wrapped the baby in swaddling cloths and laid him in "the *phátnē*," that is, in the barn in the cave below the Tower of the Flock where he was born, and where the shepherds found him, having "went quickly," Luke 2:16.

8. How many times did an angel or angels appear in connection with the overall Christmas story?

>Christmas Card Theology teaches there was one appearance of a group of God's messengers making an announcement of the birth, but ignores that the heavenly host was praising God. Christmas Card Theology also ignores all the other appearances connected to the birth. What does the Scripture say?
>
>Answer: There were a total of seven appearances of God's messengers relevant to the birth of Jesus.
>
>Explanation: Here are the seven appearances.
>
>Luke 1:11–17, to Zacharias the priest, announcing the conception of Messiah's herald, whom we know as John the Baptist.
>
>Luke 1:26–35, to Mariam of Nazareth announcing the conception of Jesus by the omnipotent power of the Holy Spirit, the one prophesied to be the Messiah-King.
>
>Matthew 1:20, to Joseph of Nazareth, revealing his fiancé Mariam of Nazareth was pregnant by the omnipotent power of the Holy Spirit with the one prophesied to be God with us and revealed to be Savior.
>
>Luke 2:9–12, to the shepherds, a single messenger announcing the birth in David's city (Bethlehem) of a Savior who is Christ (Messiah) Lord, and stating a sign by which the shepherds would recognize the baby.
>
>Luke 2:13–14, to the shepherds, with the messenger of Luke 2:9–12, many messengers praising God for the birth of the Savior and Messiah.
>
>Matthew 2:13–15, to Joseph, a messenger telling him to flee to Egypt because King Herod would try to kill Jesus.
>
>Matthew 2:19–23, to Joseph, a messenger telling him to return from Egypt to Israel, because Herod was dead.

9. What were the names of the angels who appeared to Zacharias? To Mary? To Joseph?

> Christmas Card Theology ignores the appearances to Zacharias and Joseph, and seldom gives the name of God's messenger who appeared to Mariam of Nazareth. What does the Scripture say?
>
> Answer: Luke 1:19, 26; Matthew 1:20.
>
> Explanation:
>
> To Zacharias. Luke 1:19, Gabriel, the one standing before God.
>
> To Mariam. Luke 1:26, Gabriel.
>
> To Joseph. Matthew 1:20, not named.
>
> (Although Judaism and various denominations of Christianity give individual names to many of God's messengers, the Scripture names three: Michael, who stands watch over Israel, Daniel 12:1; Gabriel, the one who stands in the presence of God, Luke 1:19; and the fallen Lucifer, Isaiah 14:12, now known as Satan.)

10. Did an angel appear first to Joseph or to Mary?

> Christmas Card Theology usually ignores the appearance of God's messenger to Joseph. What does the Scripture say?
>
> Answer: God's messenger appeared first to Mariam of Nazareth
>
> Explanation: See below
>
> Luke 1:26–38, "Now, in the sixth month, Gabriel the messenger was sent by God to a city of Galilee, whose name was Nazareth, 27 to a virgin betrothed to a man, whose name was Joseph, of the house of David; and the virgin's name was Mariam. 28 And, having come to her, he said, 'Rejoice, favored one. The Lord is with you.' 29 And at that word she was disturbed, and considered what manner this greeting might be.
>
> 30 "And the messenger said to her, 'Do not fear Mariam. For you have found favor with God. 31 Look now, you will conceive in your womb, and will bear a son, and you will call his name "Jesus." 32 He will be great, and will be called "son of Most High." And the Lord God will give him the throne of David, his father. 33 And he will reign over the house of Jacob to the ages, and of his kingdom there will not be an end.'
>
> 34 "Then said Mariam to the messenger, 'How will this be, since I know not a man?' 35 And responding the messenger said to her, 'The Holy Spirit will come upon you, and the power of Most High will rest upon you. Therefore also the holy begotten will be called, "Son of God." 36 Look now, Elizabeth, your relative, she has also conceived a son in her old age, and this month is the sixth to her who was called barren. 37 For not anything will be impossible with God.' 38 Then Mariam said, 'See the handmaid of the Lord. May it be to me according to your word.' And the messenger departed from her."
>
> Matthew 1:20–21, "But these things he [Joseph] having thought (his spirit was agitated), behold, a messenger of the Lord in a dream appeared to him, saying, 'Joseph, son of David, do not fear to receive Mariam as your wife, for that conceived in her is from the Holy Spirit. 21 She will bear a son, and you will call his name Jesus; for he will save his people from their sins.'"

11. Did the angel appear to Joseph before or after Mary was expecting the baby Jesus?

> Christmas Card Theology usually ignores the appearance of God's messenger to Joseph. What does the Scripture say?
>
> Answer: A messenger appeared to Joseph after Mariam was pregnant with Jesus.
>
> Explanation: see the scriptures in the explanation to Question 10.
>
> [Note: Yes, Questions 10 and 11 are similar. I have listed the Quiz questions according to Pastor Hollingsworth's list of questions. As every good Bible teacher knows, it helps to restate a question in a different form, to make people think and to test their understanding. Each Christmas season, Pastor Hollingsworth would choose a different set of 10–14 questions out of the 57. Question 10 was used in 1987, 1989, 2002, and 2006. Question 11 was used in 2001 and 2005.]

12. When Joseph knew Mary was pregnant, what did he initially plan to do?

>Christmas Card Theology does not mention Joseph's initial reaction to Mariam's pregnancy, just as it does not mention God's response to his initial reaction. The supra-natural does not exist in Christmas Card Theology. What does the Scripture say?
>
>Answer: Joseph decided to divorce Mariam.
>
>Explanation: Matthew 1:19, "But Joseph her husband, being righteous, and not willing to expose her publicly, desired to secretly divorce her."
>
>God's Law, as given to Israel through Moses (ca. 1445 BC), and still in effect in 6 BC when Mariam became pregnant, stated the penalty for persons discovered to have committed adultery was public execution. That same Law allowed Joseph the option of giving Mariam a certificate of divorce without stating the reason for the divorce.
>
>Joseph and Mariam were not married but engaged to be married—a betrothal. In the customs of times, a betrothal was considered as binding as a marriage, so the only way to legally dissolve a betrothal was a certificate of divorce.
>
>Joseph was a righteous man. Mariam's family had represented her as a virgin when the betrothal contract was finalized. The time between betrothal and marriage was not fixed. A girl could legally be betrothed as young as one day after her twelfth birthday. In those cases, marriage was delayed until after the onset of puberty, marked by the beginning of menstruation, after which a girl was considered a woman.
>
>[Note: if you have heard a twelve month waiting period was mandatory between betrothal and marriage, you should know that comes from rules set by sixth century AD rabbis. The New Testament, written AD 45–95, and the Mishnah, written 200 BC –AD 200, have no such rule. No such rule is known of in Gospel times.]
>
>Obviously when God's messenger Gabriel told Mariam she

would conceive and bear a child, she had reached an age and physical condition at which she could be married. In the customs of the times—in fact the custom for millennia—a female could be married any time after the onset of menstruation. For most females of the times marriage was between thirteen and fifteen years old. The same custom required a male to have financial stability before marriage, leading to males marrying in their mid to late twenties, and even as late as their early thirties.

The time between betrothal and marriage for a woman could be a little as thirty days. The time between Joseph and Mariam's betrothal and marriage is unknown, but Scripture tells us at least 90 days passed between Mariam's supra-natural conception and her marriage to Joseph, Luke 1:35–39, 56.

The natural assumption when Mariam revealed her pregnancy to Joseph was she had committed adultery—a betrothal was as binding as a marriage, but any sexual activity waited until after marriage, and therefore adultery was the likely cause of Mariam's pregnancy. The righteous thing to do was expose her adultery, an act that would take two lives, Mariam and the baby. Joseph acted righteously to preserve the life of the baby and Mariam.

The Scripture does not tell us when after the betrothal Joseph discovered Mariam was pregnant. But we know from the Scripture it was about three months after she became pregnant, Luke 1:35–40, 56. The series of events seems to be these [see Quiggle, *God Became Incarnate* for specific details].

1. In late May, as Zacharias the priest is serving in the temple, God's messenger Gabriel tells Zacharias he and his wife Elizabeth will conceive a child. The late May date is based on Luke 1:5. Every year the priestly "course of Abijah" served in the temple in late May and early December, and at the three mandatory Feasts. Each time of service was seven days, Sabbath to Sabbath. (See Question 28.)

2. Elizabeth becomes pregnant in early June after Zacharias returns home from serving in the temple.

3. In December, six months after Elizabeth becomes pregnant, God's messenger Gabriel tells Mariam she will conceive and bear a child, Luke 1:36.

4. Mariam, who lived in Nazareth of Galilee, decided to visit her relative Elizabeth, who lived in the hill country of Judea, Luke 1:29. The distance is about 100 miles.

5. At this time of year, in December, Zacharias was serving in the temple at the time of the Feast of Dedication (Hanukkah). Mariam goes to Jerusalem with relatives who are attending the Feast. There she meets her relative Zacharias, and when his time of service is completed, she goes with him to his home with Elizabeth in the hill country of Judea.

6. Mariam stays "about three months," Luke 1:56, with Elizabeth. Because Ellizabeth conceived in June, Elizabeth's pregnancy was completed in March and John was born. Mariam's stay of "about three months" was the time between the December Hanukkah and the late March or early April Passover-Unleavened Bread. Mariam was present when John was born.

7. Mariam stays "about three months," Luke 1:56, with Elizabeth. The major feast Passover-Unleavened Bread was near. All twenty-four courses of the priests served in the temple during the major feasts. After John was born Zacharias returns to Jerusalem to serve and Mariam goes with him.

8. At Passover-Unleavened Bread Mariam meets with her relatives, who came to Jerusalem for the mandatory-attendance Feast of Unleavened Bread (according to the Law, all males of a certain age had to attend Unleavened Bread). Those families attending from Nazareth caravaned together for the journey there and back, compare Luke 2:43–44.

9. Although this is speculation, it seems reasonable Mariam told Joseph she was pregnant during the three to four day return journey to Nazareth. She was by that time at the end of her first trimester, and was undoubtedly "showing" enough she could show him her "baby bump" (no silly person, not by lifting up her robes and exposing herself, but by pressing her clothing against

her stomach.)

10. Joseph is visited by an unnamed messenger of God who assures him Mariam did not commit adultery, and tells him to take Mariam as his wife. The betrothal was ended and the marriage begun after arriving in Nazareth, probably early April, 5 BC. Mariam had begun her second trimester of pregnancy.

13. Was Jesus birth a miracle?

> Christmas Card Theology usually sets aside every aspect of the miraculous and focuses on the birth. However, the birth is sometimes recognized as a miraculous virgin birth. What does the Scripture say?
>
> Answer: No, Jesus' birth was not miraculous.
>
> Explanation: Jesus' birth was as completely normal as any other human birth. Luke 2:7, "And she birthed her son, the firstborn, and swaddled him, and laid him in a barn, because there was not a place for them in the lodging."
>
> Mariam of Nazareth had a normal pregnancy and a normal delivery of the baby in her womb, with labor pains, blood, and mucus, and delivered a baby boy covered in blood and mucus, who began crying loudly, and was attached by the umbilical cord to the placenta, which followed him out of the womb. A 100% completely normal delivery.
>
> The miracle was Jesus' conception. Luke 1:34–35, "Then said Mariam to the messenger, 'How will this be, since I know not a man?' 35 And responding the messenger said to her, 'The Holy Spirit will come upon you, and the power of Most High will rest upon you. Therefore also the holy begotten will be called, 'Son of God.'"
>
> Only by ignoring or denying the accuracy, credibility, and authenticity of Luke's report can one deny the miraculous in Jesus' conception.
>
> Setting aside, only for a moment, the fact the Holy Spirit guided Luke's research and words—the Holy Spirit gave us through Luke an accurate, credible, authentic, historical, and inerrant account. Looking only at Luke's own words, 1:3, he "accurately investigated all these things from the first," in order to "write an orderly account." By "from the first" Luke means his research began at the beginning of the history.
>
> Could Luke know what happened to Zacharias, Elizabeth, Mariam, and Joseph? Luke wrote his gospel AD 58–62, while Paul was under house arrest in Procurator Felix, and later

Procurator Festus, administrative headquarters in Caesarea.

Zacharias and Elizabeth were long dead by that time, and Joseph also. However, Mariam was probably 13–15 years old when Jesus was born, making her in her early 70s when Luke interviewed her. But suppose Mariam also to be dead. Her eldest living son, James, was about 60 years of age, and pastor of the Jerusalem local church when Luke began his research. Luke did have credible sources for his gospel history—and the Holy Spirit guiding him at every step, every interview, every written word.

Luke's account of the miraculous conception and the normal birth are authentic, therefore accurate and credible.

14. Is the birth of Jesus called the immaculate conception?

Christmas Card Theology uses a Roman Catholic Church term most do not understand and wrongly apply to Jesus' birth. What does the Scripture say?

Answer: No, Jesus' birth is not the immaculate conception. Nor is Mariam's conception of Jesus (by the omnipotent power of the Holy Spirit) called the immaculate conception.

Explanation: The immaculate conception is a Roman Catholic Church doctrine that Mariam of Nazareth was conceived and born without sin and remained sinless during her life.

This doctrine had its beginning in the sixth century AD when some Roman Catholic Church theologians began teaching Mariam was born a sinner but was preserved throughout her life from sinning. In the twelfth century AD, the Roman Catholic Church began observing the Feast of the Immaculate Conception on December 8th as the month and day when Mariam was conceived in her mother's womb.

The Doctrine of the Immaculate Conception was promulgated as an Article of Faith on December 8, 1854. A Roman Catholic Church Article of Faith must be believed by a member of the Roman Catholic Church to obtain salvation.

The scripture teaches all have sinned, Romans 3:23, and only one exception, Jesus of Nazareth, who was tempted but without sin, Hebrews 4:15, see also 2 Corinthians 5:21.

Mariam implied she was a sinner when she spoke of "God my Savior, Luke 1:47. Mariam is shown sinning at Mark 3:20–21, "And he [Jesus] comes into a house, and again a crowd comes together, so that they are not even able to eat bread. 21 And having heard, his kindred [mother, brothers] went out to take him. For they said, 'He is out of his mind.'" That story continues in Mark 3:31, "And his mother came, and his brothers. And standing outside sent to him, calling him."

15. Mary and Jesus are the true Madonna and Child—yes or no?

Christmas Card Theology says Mary is the Madonna. What does the Scripture say?

Answer: No.

Explanation: the word "madonna" was a 16th century AD term used as a respectful way to speak of or to an Italian woman. In the 17th century AD the Roman Catholic Church adopted "Madonna" as one of several titles for Mariam of Nazareth.

A "Madonna and Child" has a long history in ancient paganism. For example, the Egyptian god Isis and her child Osiris-Horus; the Greco-Roman god Venus-Aphrodite and her child Eros-Cupid; the Chinese god Shimagoo, the German god Hertha, the Scandinavian god Disa, the Etruscan god Nutria, the Druid god Virgo, the Sumerian god Nana. The Asian god Cybele (the Great Mother of the gods; the mother-goddess) and her child Deoius; and many more.

In every instance the Mother and child were both worshiped as gods. In the Roman Catholic Church, worship of Mariam alongside Jesus Christ began AD 431 and became fixed in regular worship practices in AD 788.

For many years there has been a movement in the Roman Catholic Church to declare as an Article of Faith Mary of Nazareth as Co-Redemptrix with Christ. The term "Co-Redemptrix" is defined in two ways: one way by the laity, one way by Roman Catholic Church dogma.

The Laity. In my library I have a small book, dated May 6, 1993, by Mark I. Miravalle, titled, *Mary, Coredemptrix, Mediatrix, Advocate."* The book has the Nihil Obstat and Imprimatur indicating it is an officially authorized publication of the Roman Catholic Church. The book comes with two postcards addressed to the Pope, asking him to "define as Christian dogma the Church's constant teaching on Mary's co redemptive (*sic*) role with Christ as the Redeemer of humanity."

The Roman Catholic Church began to realize their "constant teaching on Mary's co redemptive (*sic*) role" was opposed by

Protestants and others, hindering Roman Catholic Church efforts at ecumenism. A change was made.

Dogma. The current official dogma of the Roman Catholic Church on this subject is Mary "is a woman who cooperates with the Redeemer" similar to the way all Christians cooperate with the Redeemer, and "Co-Redemptrix, is no longer being treated by the Magisterium as an authoritative expression of Catholic doctrine." [Source, Catholic Answers, catholic.com]

The current Pope Francis, in 2019, speaking about the theology of Mary as co-redemptrix, declared "She never introduced herself as co-redemptrix," and declared that dogma "foolishness." Others, including Archbishop Carlo Maria Viganò (Letter #65, 2019: Viganò on Francis and Mary), disagreed. Vigano wrote, "Those who 'hybridize' and profane them [that is, these Marian dogmas] show that they are on the side of the Enemy. Attacking Mary is attacking Christ himself."

In genuine Christianity there are no confusing terms, or encouragement to worship Mary. Only Jesus Christ is worshiped, because only Jesus Christ is the God-man Redeemer.

Mariam is not the Madonna and is not a co-redemptrix.

16. Was Jesus born in Galilee, Samaria, or Judea?

>Christmas Card Theology teaches Jesus was born in Bethlehem, but the location of Bethlehem is not revealed. Many subscribing to Christmas Card Theology do not know. What does the Scripture say?
>
>Answer: Galilee, Samaria, and Judea were administrative regions (think states or counties) in ancient Roman-controlled Israel, which was a small part of the larger Imperial Province Syria. Jesus was born in Judea and lived in Galilee.
>
>Explanation: Luke 2:4–6, "Then also Joseph went up from Galilee, out of the town of Nazareth, to Judea, to the city of David, which is called Bethlehem, because he was of the house and family of David, 5 to register, with Mariam, the one being betrothed to him, she being with child. 6 Then it happened in their being there, the days of her giving birth were fulfilled."
>
>Matthew 21:21–22," Now Joseph got up, took the child and his mother, and came into the land of Israel. 22 But having heard that Archelaus rules Judea in place of his father Herod, he was afraid to go there. Having been warned by God in a dream, he turned in to the region of Galilee."
>
>Luke 2:39, "And when they had completed all according to the Law of the Lord, they returned to Galilee, to their town Nazareth."
>
>In 930 BC, Solomon's kingdom split into two kingdoms after his death. The southern Kingdom was known as Judah, the northern Kingdom was known as Israel-Samaria. The northern kingdom was ended in 733 BC by the Assyrian Empire, but the name for the region stuck. The southern kingdom ended for seventy years in 609 BC with the Babylonian Captivity. When the 70 years were completed, some of the Jews returned and remade Judah (the name "Jew" originated in Babylon, the "captives of Jew-dah"), which later became known as Judea, the land of the Jews.
>
>Judea is south of Samaria, Galilee is north of Samaria. The name "Galilee" seems to mean region of the gentiles. The first mention of Galilee is Joshua 20:7. The region was initially

associated with the territory given to the tribe of Napthali.

17. By what means of conveyance (mode of transportation) did Joseph and Mary travel to Bethlehem for Jesus' Birth?

>Christmas Card Theology teaches Mary rode a donkey. What does the Scripture say?

>Answer: The Scripture does not say.

>Explanation: See Question 18.

18. Did Mary ride a donkey from Nazareth to Bethlehem?

Christmas Card Theology teaches Mariam rode a donkey. What does the Scripture say?

Answer: The Scripture does not say, but Scripture and secular history give information that allows us to construct a reasonable answer.

Explanation: Every fourteen years (see Question 21), beginning in 23 BC, Rome began taking a census of all the property owners in the Roman Empire for taxation purposes. Of course, that meant mostly males, as very few women held property in their own name.

Joseph was a carpenter (or stone mason). Here is where the story overlaps with Question 20. Both Jospeh and Mariam knew the Old Testament scriptures. They knew the heir of David, Luke 1:32, must be born in Bethlehem. So they were making a permanent move to Bethlehem (see Question 21 for the other reasons Mariam went with Joseph).

Because they were making a permanent move to Bethlehem, Joseph had to bring all his tools and supplies, as well as their household goods. Joseph put everything in the cart he used for his business and hitched his donkey to the cart. Joseph, the donkey, and the very pregnant Mary walked to Bethlehem from Nazareth.

Mariam didn't ride the donkey—it was pulling the cart full of their stuff. Mariam walked.

Mariam was very pregnant, so they may not have walked very far each day. We are going to be very considerate of Mariam and not make her walk ten hours a day at a pace of three miles per hour. There was no need to hurry. The Holy Spirit would have moved them out and along to be there on time and in the right place when the time came for Mariam to deliver her baby. They made the best and most reasonable time they could.

So the first day they probably left Nazareth late (last minute packing and goodbyes), walked the eighteen miles to Scythopolis (six to seven hours), and stopped for the night. The second day they started for Shechem in Samaria, about 35 miles south of Scythopolis, probably stopping at some little village along the way. The third day they completed the trip to Shechem and rested for the night. The fourth day they began the trip to Jerusalem from Shechem, about 35 miles, probably stopping at some little village along the way.

When they arrived at Jerusalem the fifth day of the journey, they may have spent the night, or continued on and walked the 5 miles to Bethlehem. If they walked a little faster it might have taken them three to four days from Nazareth to Bethlehem. Because Mariam was very pregnant, and they knew the child must be born in Bethlehem, one can assume they made the best time and distance possible for her advanced condition.

The most likely answer is Mariam did not ride a donkey but walked the 100 miles or so to Bethlehem in five to seven days. If this seems unrealistic to you, remember, in those times everyone walked to wherever they wanted to go. Horses were for the very rich, Roman military officers, and high-ranking government officials. Donkeys and camels were for commerce, not personal transportation. People, even very pregnant people, were physically conditioned by daily life to be able to walk wherever they wanted to go, even a hundred miles when very pregnant.

[Note: Joseph's occupation. In Matthew 13:35 Joseph's occupation is said to be *téktōn* [Zodhiates, s. v. 5045]. Older language studies concluded this word meant "an artificer, a craftsman, especially a worker in wood." More recent language studies have indicated this word described a builder, probably working in stone.]

19. Why was Mary's baby to be named Jesus, according to the angel?

> Christmas Card Theology doesn't quite tell us why Mariam's baby boy was to be named Jesus. What does the Scripture say?
>
> Answer: Mariam's baby was to be named "Jesus" because both Joseph and Mariam were told to name the child "Jesus."
>
> Explanation: Luke 1:30–31, "And the messenger said to her, 'Do not fear Mariam. For you have found favor with God. 31 Look now, you will conceive in your womb, and will bear a son, and you will call his name 'Jesus.'"
>
> Matthew 1:20–21, "But these things he having thought (his spirit was agitated), behold, a messenger of the Lord in a dream appeared to him, saying, 'Joseph, son of David, do not fear to receive Mariam as your wife, for that conceived in her is from the Holy Spirit. 21 She will bear a son, and you will call his name Jesus; for he will save his people from their sins.'"
>
> What is notable here is in the culture of the times the father named the child, see Luke 1:59–63. Who named Jesus? Joseph officially named his stepson "Jesus" per the commandment he had been given by God's messenger. Jesus' father, God, gave him the name "Jesus."
>
> In Matthew's gospel, the messenger states a reason the child would be named Jesus: "for he will save his people from their sins." The Greek name *Iēsoús*, which has been transliterated as "Jesus," is the Greek form of the Hebrew *Yēshūa*, which means "YHWH his help." The help *Yēshūa* will give is to save his people from their sins.

20. Considering that Joseph and Mary lived in Nazareth, why did Jesus come to be born in Bethlehem?

>Christmas Card Theology teaches nothing on this subject. What does the Scripture say?
>
>Answer: To fulfill prophecy.
>
>Explanation: Micah 5:2 (LXX), "And thou, Bethleem, house of Ephratha, art few in number to be reckoned among the thousands of Juda; yet out of thee shall one come forth to me, to be a ruler of Israel; and his goings forth were from the beginning, even from eternity."
>
>It would be unreasonable to believe Joseph and Mariam did not know the Micah 5:2 prophecy. Messianic prophecy was taught in the synagogue schools in every village with a synagogue, a school Joseph attended as a minor child. The topic of messianic prophecy was a subject taught by those preaching in the synagogue services which Mariam attended (women were not allowed to attend the synagogue school).
>
>The Micah 5:2 prophecy was the first reason Joseph and Mariam left Nazareth for Bethlehem, so Jesus would be born in Bethlehem. See Question 21 for the second and third reasons.

21. What was the reason, or reasons, Joseph and Mary left Nazareth and went to Bethlehem?

>Christmas Card Theology does not say why Joseph and Mariam left Nazareth and went to Bethlehem. What does the Scripture say?
>
>Answer: There were three reasons Joseph and Mariam left Nazareth and went to Bethlehem. The first was Micah 5:2 (see Question 20). The second reason was the Roman census. The third reason was their marriage in the second trimester of her pregnancy.
>
>Explanation:
>
>Prophecy. Micah 5:2 was discussed at Questions 6, 20.
>
>The census. Luke 2:1–5, "Now it happened in those times, a decree went out from Caesar Augustus to register all the world in a census. 2 And this earlier enrollment took place when Quirinius was Procurator in Syria. 3 And all were going to be registered, each to their city. 4 Then also Joseph went up from Galilee, out of the town of Nazareth, to Judea, to the city of David, which is called Bethlehem, because he was of the house and family of David, 5 to register, with Mariam, the one being betrothed to him, she being with child."
>
>[For a discussion of Quirinius as the Procurator-Legate of Caesar (not governor as in the KJV) see my book *God Became Incarnate*, or see Ramsay, *Was Christ Born in Bethlehem*.]
>
>Mariam did not need to go to Bethlehem with Joseph for the census. Only adult male property owners would be counted. Joseph had a business (carpentry, or more likely stone mason) and so must pay taxes. Joseph and Mariam, knowing Micah 5:2, used the census to give their relatives their reason for moving to Bethlehem.
>
>The census mentioned in Luke 2:1 was scheduled for 9 BC, which meant the actual counting would be done in 8 BC (a year was spent in administrative preparation).
>
>For reasons much too complex to fully discuss here (see *God Became Incarnate*) King Herod, who had been collecting Roman

taxes in Israel in his own name (and then paying them to Rome) was forced to collect taxes in Rome's name; Herod had been stripped of his "Friend of Caesar" political status, which took away several privileges he had enjoyed as King.

Herod feared a revolt against Rome if the census was done in Rome's name (which happened at the next census in AD 6, Acts 5:37). Herod decided to disguise the tax collection census by conducting it by tribal affiliation, like the census conducted in the book of Numbers. That meant all the males with property had to go to their tribal hometown. That meant Joseph had to travel to Bethlehem because he was of the family of David of the tribe of Judah, Matthew 1:20; Luke 2:2.

The third reason Mariam went with Joseph to live in Bethlehem, is Mariam did not marry Joseph until early April, about three months after she conceived in December, Luke 1:35–40, 56. At the time of their move to Bethlehem, nine months after her conception, Mariam was obviously more pregnant than five months of marriage from late April or early May would require. There was undoubtedly a lot of gossip about Mary's due date.

By giving birth away from Nazareth, Jesus would be assumed to have been born nine months from their wedding, and the families and the child would be spared social embarrassment. Joseph wasn't just responding to the census, he and Mariam were moving to Bethlehem to rent a house (Matthew 2:8–11), have the baby (Micah 4:8, 5:2), and live in Bethlehem.

22. Of what Hebrew tribe were Joseph and Mary?

>Christmas Card Theology does not teach this information. In fact, modern Christmas Card Theology tends to skip over the fact Joseph, Mariam, and Jesus were Hebrews (Jews). What does the Scripture say?

>Answer: Joseph and Mariam were of the Hebrew tribe of Judah.

>Explanation:

>Joseph's lineage. Matthew 1:1–16, "Book of the genealogy of Jesus Christ, son of David, son of Abraham.

>>$_2$ "Abraham fathered Isaac; and Isaac fathered Jacob; and Jacob fathered Judah and his brothers; $_3$ and Judah fathered Perez and Zerah of Tamar; and Perez fathered Hezron; and Hezron fathered Ram; $_4$ and Ram fathered Amminadab; and Amminadab fathered Nahshon; and Nahshon fathered Salmon; $_5$ and Salmon fathered Boaz of Rahab; and Boaz fathered Obed of Ruth; and Obed fathered Jesse; $_6$ and Jesse fathered David the king.

>>"And David the king fathered Solomon of her of Uriah; $_7$ and Solomon fathered Rehoboam; and Rehoboam fathered Abijah; and Abijah fathered Asa; $_8$ and Asa fathered Jehoshaphat; and Jehoshaphat fathered Joram; and Joram fathered Uzziah; $_9$ and Uzziah fathered Jotham; and Jotham fathered Ahaz; and Ahaz fathered Hezekiah; $_{10}$ and Hezekiah fathered Manasseh; and Manasseh fathered Amon; and Amon fathered Josiah. $_{11}$ and Josiah fathered Jeconiah and his brothers at the time of the relocation to Babylon.

>>$_{12}$ "And after the relocation to Babylon Jeconiah fathered Shealtiel; and Shealtiel fathered Zerubbabel; $_{13}$ and Zerubbabel fathered Abiud; and Abiud fathered Eliakim, and Eliakim fathered Azor; $_{14}$ and Azor fathered Zadok; and Zadok fathered Achim; and Achim fathered Eliud; $_{15}$ and Eliud fathered Eleazar; and Eleazar fathered Matthan; and Matthan fathered Jacob; $_{16}$ and Jacob fathered Joseph the husband of Mariam, of whom was born Jesus, the one named Christ."

> Luke 2:4, "Then also Joseph went up from Galilee, out of the town of Nazareth, to Judea, to the city of David, which is called Bethlehem, because he was of the house and family of David."

Mariam's lineage.

Luke does not directly state Mariam's lineage, because in the culture of the times no one cared about a woman's lineage. But Luke cared, and the Holy Spirit cared. If one compares Matthew's lineage of Joseph, specifically Matthew 1:16, with Luke's genealogy, specifically Luke 3:23, a difference is immediately apparent.

> Matthew 1:15–16, "and Matthan fathered Jacob, and Jacob fathered Joseph the husband of Mariam, of whom was born Jesus, the one named Christ."

> Luke 3:23, "And Jesus himself was beginning about thirty years, being son, as was supposed, of Joseph of Heli, of Matthat."

Joseph cannot at the same time physically be the son of Jacob and the son of Heli. Several solutions are proposed, among them a second marriage of the mother to Heli, or a levirate marriage to the mother by Jacob's brother Heli. Both solutions suppose Mariam to be the daughter of Heli, but if so not from Joseph's mother, for then the marriage of Joseph and Mariam would violate Leviticus 18:9.

Whatever the solution to Joseph's two fathers, the solution to the two lineages is Matthew gives Joseph's physical lineage and Luke gives Mariam's physical lineage. That solution makes sense when Matthew 1:7 is compared with Luke 3:31.

> Matthew 1:7, "and Solomon fathered Rehoboam"

> Luke 3:31, "of Nathan, of David, 32 of Jesse"

Matthew gives Joseph's decent as from Rehoboam son of David. Luke gives Mariam's descent as from Nathan son of David. Matthew gives the royal descent of the Christ through Joseph, but Luke gives the physical descent of the

Christ through Mariam.

Luke 3:23–38, "And Jesus himself was beginning about thirty years, being son, as was supposed, of Joseph of Heli, 24 of Matthat, of Levi, of Melchi, of Jannai, of Joseph, 25 of Mattathias, of Amos, of Nahum, of Hesli, of Naggai, 26 of Maath, of Mattathias, of Semein, of Josech, of Joda, 27 of Joanan, of Rhesa, of Zorobabel, of Salathiel, of Nen, 28 of Melchi, of Addi, of Kosam, of Elmadam, of Er, 29 of Joshua, of Eliezer, of Jorim, of Matthat, of Levi, 30 of Simeon, of Judah, of Joseph, of Jonam, of Eliakim, 31 of Melea, of Menna, of Mattatha, of Nathan, of David, 32 of Jesse, of Obed, of Boaz, of Sala, of Naasson, 33 of Aminadab, of Admin, of Arni, of Hezron, of Perez, of Judah, of Jacob, of Isaac, of Abraham, of Terah, of Nahor, 35 of Serouch, of Rhagau, of Peleg, of Eber, of Sala, 36 of Kainan, of Arphaxad, of Shem, of Noah, of Lamech, 37 of Methuselah, of Enoch, of Jared, of Mahalalel, of Kainam, 38 of Enos, of Seth, of Adam, of God."

Both royal and physical lineage support both Joseph and Mariam being of the tribe of Judah. Joseph is descended from David's son Solomon. Mariam is descended from David's son Nathan.

23. Did Joseph legally wed Mary before or after the birth of Jesus?

> Christmas Card Theology teaches nothing about the betrothal or marriage of Joseph and Mariam. What does the Scripture say?
>
> Answer: Joseph legally wed Mariam before the birth of Jesus.
>
> Explanation: Matthew 1:24–25, "Then Joseph, being aroused from sleep, did as the messenger of the Lord commanded him and took to him his wife, 25 and did not know her until she had brought forth her firstborn son. And he called his name Jesus."
>
> Joseph and Mariam were married soon after Mariam told Joseph she had become pregnant by the omnipotent power of the Holy Spirit. Joseph did not believe her—who would?—but God sent one of his messengers (unnamed) who said to Joseph, Matthew 1:20, "Joseph, son of David, do not fear to receive Mariam as your wife, for that conceived in her is from the Holy Spirit."

24. When was the name "Jesus" first given to the child to be born of Mary?

> Christmas Card Theology occasionally rearranges Luke 1:31 into "his name shall be called Jesus," but the messenger's announcement and the miraculous conception are not mentioned. What does the Scripture say?
>
> Answer: the name "Jesus" was first given to Mariam, at the announcement of his conception.
>
> Explanation: Mariam was the first person to know she would conceive and birth the prophesied Messiah. Joesph was told, by Mariam, about three months later, Luke 1:39, 56.
>
> Luke 1:31, "Look now, you [Mariam] will conceive in your womb, and will bear a son, and you will call his name 'Jesus.'"

25. When was the name "Jesus" given a second time to the child to be born of Mary?

> Christmas Card Theology ignores the second time. What does the Scripture say?
>
> Answer: the name "Jesus" was given a second time to Joseph.
>
> Explanation: Miriam, immediately after being told she would conceive and birth the Messiah, Luke 1:31, left her home in Nazareth and visited her relative Elizabeth in the hill country of Judea, Luke 1:39, for about three months, Luke 1:56. Joseph learned of Mariam's pregnancy during or after her return to Nazareth from visiting Elizabeth, Matthew 1:18 (see Question 12).
>
> Matthew 1:21, "She [Mariam] will bear a son, and you [Joseph] will call his name Jesus; for he will save his people from their sins."
>
> Matthew 1:24 states "Then Joseph, being aroused from sleep [i.e., waking up from the dream visitation of 1:20–21] did as the messenger of the Lord commanded him and took to him his wife."

The sequence of events strongly implies Joseph married Mariam within a short time after waking from the dream-visitation.

The most reasonable view that fits the facts of Scripture is the announcement to Mariam, Mariam's visit to Elizabeth, Mariam's return to Nazareth, Joseph's dream-visitation (during or immediately after the return to Nazareth from Passover-Unleavened Bread), Joseph marries Mariam.

Passover-Unleavened bread took place during the eight days from April 20 to April 28, 5 BC. Joseph married Mariam in late April or early May, 5 BC. She was in her second trimester.

26. When did Mary's first-born child actually receive his name legally and officially?

> Christmas Card Theology knows he was named "Jesus" but is not concerned with the culture of the times that determined when to give a legal name. What does the Scripture say?
>
> Answer: Mariam's first-born child received his name legally and officially at his circumcision, according to the customs of the times.
>
> Explanation: Luke 2:21, "And when eight days were fulfilled to circumcise him, then he was called his name, Jesus, which had been called by the messenger before he was conceived in the womb."
>
> There was not a scriptural or legal reason to delay naming a child, but a cultural reason. In those days infant mortality was high. For example, Roman culture did not give a child a Roman name (a Roman name had three parts as per legal rules for naming; modern Iceland retains this custom, restricting what name a child may be legally named). In the Greco-Roman culture of the times, infant and child mortality was so high a child did not receive his or her legal Roman name until five years old.
>
> In the Israel of Joseph and Mariam, the naming delay for a male child was eight days after birth, when a male child was required to be circumcised, according to the Abrahamic and Mosaic covenants.
>
> Then, thirty-three days after the male child was circumcised, he was officially presented to the Lord in the temple with an appropriate sacrifice, Leviticus 12:4, 6–8.
>
> A female child was not circumcised (female circumcision is a barbaric custom practiced into modern times by some cultures). A female child was presented to the Lord after sixty-six days with an appropriate sacrifice, Leviticus 12:5–8.

27. What month and year was Jesus born?

   Christmas Card Theology teaches December 25. The year is not mentioned. What does the Scripture say?

   Answer: Scripture does not explicitly say.

   Explanation: Some early Church fathers, and Roman Catholic Church tradition, say Jesus was born December 25. The world has accepted that date as the official month and day.

   Augustine (AD 354–430) is often cited as a source for the December 25 date. "For He is believed to have been conceived on the 25th of March," ["On the Trinity," 4.5]. Nine months after 25 March is 25 December.

   However, Augustine did not knew the conception date, but was trying to make an allegory between conception on March 25 and crucifixion on March 25, "so the womb of the virgin, in which he was conceived ... corresponds to the new grave in which he was buried" [same reference]. However, today we know Jesus was crucified, died, and was buried on April 4, AD 33 (see vol. 2 of my commentary on John's gospel, Appendix.)

   Scripture does tell us Jesus was born before Herod died, Matthew 2:1. Secular history tells us Herod died shortly after an eclipse of the moon on March 12, 4 BC. The Passover on April 11, 4 BC was celebrated after his death. Herod died in the thirty-fourth year of his reign, which began March 29, 4 BC. So Herod died between March 29 and April 11, 4 BC.

   Matthew's Gospel says Herod was alive when Jesus was born. A new year began fourteen days before Passover (Passover was April 11 in 4 BC), so the new year of 4 BC began on March 28. Herod died between March 29 and April 11, 4 BC. Jesus was born in 5 BC before Herod died.

   One should remember that the years designated "BC" count down, not up. For example, 7 BC became 6 BC, which became 5 BC, which became 4 BC. Also, there is no year zero in the BC system. For example, the year AD 1999 became the year AD 2000 and a year later became AD 2001. In the BC counting system, the year 1 BC became the year AD 1.

Herod died a few days after the year 5 BC became 4 BC, so Jesus was born in 5 BC. Most bible scholars believe Jesus was born between 7 BC–4 BC. I have explained and defended a 5 BC birth year in my book *God Became Incarnate.*

Before he died, Herod met with the Magi, and afterward sent soldiers to kill all the children in the region of Bethlehem, two years old or younger. If the "star" the Magi saw began its illumination the day Jesus was born, that means several months had passed before the Magi met with Herod—sufficient time for Joseph to move his family into a house in Bethlehem, where the Magi found them, Matthew 2:9–11.

As to the month Jesus was born see Question 28.

For the Magi and the "star" see Question 49.

28. Why is it reasonable to assume Jesus was not born in December?

Christmas Card Theology does not admit the possibility of other than a December birth. What does the Scripture say?

Answer: Scripture and secular history give evidence from which a reasonable answer may be developed.

Explanation: What help does the Scripture and secular history give us? I tell the complete story in my books, *God Became Incarnate* and *The Christmas Story, As Told by God*. Here I have space for an abbreviated version of the full story. The full story is on pages 90–103 of *God Became Incarnate*.

The enrollment for the 9 BC census, Luke 2:1, was scheduled to be conducted in 8 BC (a year was given for administrative preparation). But in Herod's kingdom it was probably delayed for some time, because in 9 BC Herod had invaded a neighboring country (Josephus, *Antiquities*, 16.9.2). In response Caesar said that "henceforth he would treat him as a subject," meaning Herod had lost his political status, "Friend of Caesar."

With the loss of status, Herod was required to conduct the enrollment and collect the taxes in the name of Rome. He knew that if he conducted the enrollment-taxation in the name of Rome there might be a rebellion. The Jews hated the Romans and believed their taxes should not support their Roman oppressors. The next enrollment in AD 6 (mentioned in Acts 5:37) was conducted under Roman authority and there was a minor rebellion.

Herod delayed the census for at least two years as he tried to regain his "Friend of Caesar" status, without success. You need to understand the process. All travel was on land by foot, and on water by sailing vessels used to carry cargo, with stops at many ports along the way (compare Acts 20:13–21:7; 27:1–28:13). Herod was under the immediate jurisdiction of the governor of the Imperial Syrian Province. He sent a delegation to the governor for permission to appeal to Caesar in Rome: a round trip of 629 km or 391 miles, by foot, or about 4–5 weeks round trip. Having received permission, Herod sent a delegation to Rome, 4,044 km or 2,513 miles to get there, by foot and sail-driven cargo boat, a journey of several months (compare Paul's trip as a prisoner sent to Rome, Acts 27–28). The delegation waited in Rome for weeks; Caesar refused to see them. Another 4,044 km or 2,513 miles to return. The delegation returned empty handed. Herod tried again, same process, same result. More than a year—possibly close to two years—passed with both attempts.

Having lost his appeal to regain his status, Herod had to decide how to conduct a Roman enrollment in a way that would not incite rebellion. Keeping the peace had high priority in the policy of *Pax Romana* (obeying Roman laws, paying Roman taxes, worshiping Roman gods). Herod decided to enroll the Jews using the old tribal system, the way the people were numbered in the Old Testament. The enrollment would then seem as though it was a Jewish idea, not a Roman requirement. Every Jew knew his tribe and the main city of his tribe, so an enrollment by tribal affiliation was reasonable to the Jews.

Having decided how to conduct the enrollment, Herod had to delay it a second time to get Caesar Augustus' permission to use a non-Roman method. He again had to get permission from the Syrian governor, by this time Governor Varus (7–4 BC). The governor gave permission to see Augustus, and Augustus received this delegation and gave permission to conduct the enrollment according to Jewish tradition. About another year passed.

Bottom line? In his attempt to regain his "Friend of Caesar" status, Herod sent two delegations to the Syrian governor and two delegations to Caesar in Rome. Two round-trips between Jerusalem and Damascus (for the Roman governor's permission), plus two roundtrips between Jerusalem and Rome (to see Caesar), plus time expended in the administrative and logistic actions required to make the journeys, plus waiting for appointments with the Syrian governor and with Caesar, would have consumed more than one year, probably two. It was probably mid-to-late 6 BC when the third delegation was sent—first to the Syrian governor, then to Rome—and returned to tell Herod he had been given permission to conduct the enrollment according to the old tribal method.

Having received permission, Herod must now decide when to conduct the enrollment. Even if the date was late 7 BC or early to mid-6 BC, there were administrative issues to be resolved: contracts to let to tax-collectors, lodging to arrange for collectors and government officials, public announcements to be written, copied, posted, and proclaimed, and all the other little things necessary to conduct a nation-wide government operation—all to be accomplished by foot and hand, requiring months of preparation.

If the date of Caesar's approval was mid to late 6 BC, Elizabeth was already pregnant (see below). The winter months of 6 BC would be difficult because the weather was cold and rainy from December through February (Mariam was now pregnant, see below). The spring and summer months of 5 BC (Mariam and Joseph were married, see below) would create economic hardship.

Israel was an agrarian economy. The barley harvest began in late March, and the wheat harvest in late May. Millet, flax, and sesame were harvested in July. The grape harvest began in July [Borowski, 37]. Grain was not completely threshed and stored until the end of July. To have the head of every house report to the city of his tribe at any time from March through July might have plunged the nation into economic chaos and famine. So it seems likely Herod selected August through October, 5 BC as the best time for the enrollment.

Here is where the story intersects with Scripture. Luke 1:5 says Zacharias (the man who would be John the Baptist's father) was a priest in the division of Abijah, known as the eighth division. The priests served in the temple in a rotation known as courses or divisions. About 1,000 BC, David the king, with Zadok and Ahimelech the priests, divided the sons of Aaron into twenty-four divisions, 1 Chronicles 24:1–19. Each priest served in their division two times during the year, for one week each time, from one Sabbath to the next. But during the three mandatory Feasts all the divisions served together.

The divisions began their rotation at the start of the religious year, Nisan 1 (Nisan corresponds to the modern March-April).

In 6 BC the division would have been as follows [Quiggle and Hollingsworth, *Chronology*, 23].

First division, Nisan 1–8 (March 20–27), 6 BC.

Second division, Nisan 8–15 (March 27–April 3), 6 BC.

All the priests served Nisan 15–31 (April 3–9), 6 BC for Unleavened Bread.

Third division, Nisan 22–29 (April 10–17), 6 BC.

Fourth division, Nisan 29–Iyyar 6 (April 17–24), 6 BC.

Fifth division, Iyyar 6–13 (April 24–May 1), 6 BC.

Sixth division, Iyyar 13–20 (May 1–18), 6 BC.

Seventh division, Iyyar 20–27 (May 8–15), 6 BC.

All the priests served Iyyar 27–Sivan 5 (May 15–22), 6 BC for Pentecost.

Eighth division, Sivan 5–12 (May 22–29), 6 BC.

The scriptures relating to the eighth division served by Zacharias in 6 BC are Luke 1:5; 1 Chronicles 24:3–5, 10.

According to Luke, Elizabeth became pregnant after Zacharias returned from his temple service. That would be June, 6 BC. Six months later would be December, 6 BC. Mariam conceived in December, Luke 1:36, and immediately visited Elizabeth in the sixth month of Elizabeth's pregnancy. Elizabeth conceived in June, 6 BC, so John the Baptist was born about 270 days later, in March, 5 BC. (The new year began in March.)

Mariam stayed with Elizabeth for "about three months," Luke 1:56, i.e., from mid-December to about mid-March. Mariam saw John born, returned to Jerusalem with Zacharias, returned to Nazareth with relatives, and probably told Joseph she was pregnant during the Jerusalem-to-Nazareth trip (see Question 12). Mariam married Joseph upon her return to Nazareth in late April or early May, 5 BC.

If Mariam conceived between December 1–3, 6 BC, then a normal 270–271 day pregnancy means her gestation period would have ended at the earliest about August 30, 5 BC. Normal variations in the gestation period would allow for a late August to early September, 5 BC birth. The biblical and secular data supports the 5 BC date. When Herod met with the wise men Jesus was living in a house in Bethlehem.

There is perhaps a biblical notice of the time of year. The Feast of Tabernacles was Saturday, September 16 through Saturday, September 23 in 5 BC. Jesus was born three to four weeks before Tabernacles, was circumcised eight days later (Luke 2:21), and thirty-three days after that (Leviticus 12:2–8), Simeon and Anna saw him in the Temple, Luke 2:25–38. John 1:14 says, "And the Word became embodied and dwelt among us. And we saw his glory—glory as of a one and only begotten with the Father, full of grace and truth." That word "dwelt" translates the Greek word *skēnóō*, literally a tent, a tabernacle. "And the Word became embodied and *skēnóō*, tabernacled, among us."

The scriptural and secular evidence supports the reasonable conclusion Jesus was born in 5 BC about the end of August or early September.

29. Did someone (an innkeeper?) provide or send Joseph and Mary to a stable?

> Christmas Card Theology sometimes (in a movie or TV special) has some wretched innkeeper turning the couple away. What does the Scripture say?
>
> Answer: The Scripture does not say, because there was no innkeeper.
>
> Explanation: Luke 2:7, "And she birthed her son, the firstborn, and swaddled him, and laid him in a barn, because there was not a place for them in the lodging."
>
> The word I translated "lodging" is in many English versions "inn."
>
> In Question 7, I mentioned the English "inn" was a mistranslation. The Greek word is *katáluma*, which in New Testament times could be a guest room in a house, an open area surrounded by a wall with niches in the wall for people and animals, or a large open area set aside for people to camp for the night.
>
> There was no inn, there was no innkeeper. At the very most, if they had been seeking accommodations in a guest room, the owner of the house might have suggested another form of *katáluma*. But no one would have suggested the place where shepherds kept sheep, because shepherds were considered ceremonially unclean, and all those seeing a pregnant woman about to deliver would not have suggested the shepherd's *phátnē*, aka: stable, barn. (See Question 7.)
>
> Joseph and the very pregnant Mariam did not find a *katáluma* in Bethlehem because all such were full of people come to enroll in the census. This was God's plan, and I believe the Holy Spirit prompted Micah 4:8 to their memory, sending them to the Tower of the Flock. Certainly the use of *phátnē* as the place where Jesus was born suggests the Tower of the Flock was the scriptural alternate to an unavailable *katáluma*, as per Micah 4:8. See Question 7. The world romanticizes the Christmas story. The Scripture presents the reality. Which will you believe?

30. Did Mary know exactly who her son, Jesus, was?

> Christmas Card Theology does not say anything about this and certainly does not say how she knew. What does the Scripture say?

Answer: Yes … and no.

Explanation: Luke 1:31–33, "Look now, you will conceive in your womb, and will bear a son, and you will call his name 'Jesus.' 32 He will be great, and will be called 'son of Most High.' And the Lord God will give him the throne of David, his father. 33 And he will reign over the house of Jacob to the ages, and of his kingdom there will not be an end."

The messenger Gabriel repeats the prophecy given in 2 Samuel 7:8, 13, 16 (LXX).

> And now thus shalt thou say to my servant David …
>
> He [the coming one] shall build for me a house to my name, and I will set up his throne even for ever.
>
> And his [the coming one] house shall be made sure, and his kingdom for ever before me, and his throne shall be set up for ever.

Mariam knew, because the messenger Gabriel told her, that her child Jesus would inherit the promise made to David of a house (descendants), throne (dominion), and kingdom (land and those to be ruled) forever. We know that is how David understood the prophecy, because that is what he tells us in Psalm 2.

> 2:2, an anointed (Hebrew: *māshîah*)
>
> 2:6, King of Israel
>
> 2:7, son of Most High
>
> 2:8-12, King of the nations

This is the promise of Messiah-King and his unending kingdom. The Old Testament peoples—all persons in the four gospels are Old Testament peoples—would have thought of an unending line of descendants to rule in an unending kingdom. They had centuries of the descendants of David ruling Judah to validate their understanding of the prophecy. We who have received the New Testament revelation have a different view of an unending kingdom. The testimony in the New Testament tells us Jesus Christ is God incarnate. But we cannot read that understanding into a time when all people had was the Old Testament revelation.

Pastor Hollingsworth's answer also gives Luke 1:47. But in this he was wrong. Let us look at 1:46–48, And Mariam said, "My soul is praising the Lord, 47 and my spirit rejoices in God my savior, 48 for he had regard unto the humble state of his handmaiden."

Just who was it who had "regard unto the humble state of his handmaiden." Look at Luke 1:30, And the messenger said to her, "Do not fear Mariam. For you have found favor with God." The "Lord" in 1:46 is YHWH, and "my Savior" in 1:47 is YHWH, and "he" and "his" in 1:48 are YHWH. Not her newly conceived and yet to be born child Jesus, but the same YHWH she and her Hebrew ancestors had worshiped and depended upon for salvation.

Pastor Hollingsworth made the same error almost all believers make today: that certain people knew Jesus of Nazareth was God the Son incarnate. No they did not. Many believed Jesus was the Messian-King. Only a close, intimate handful believed Jesus was the Messiah-Redeemer (perhaps Mary of Bethany who anointed him for his burial before he died, John 12:3–7).

During the time from Jesus' conception to his death and burial no one believed Jesus was God incarnate. That would violate 1,500 years of "Hear O Israel, YHWH our God, YHWH is one," Deuteronomy 6:4. The Trinity of one God, three persons, was not as developed in the Old Testament as it is in the New Testament. The evidence is in the Old Testament, but we understand that evidence because of the New Testament revelation.

During Gospel times, during the time of Jesus Christ's public ministry between his baptism and ascension, the people were evaluating Jesus to see if he was Messiah-King who would redeem the nation Israel from gentile oppression. That is what Mariam thought, Luke 1:52. That is what Zacharias thought, Luke 1:71, 74. That is what John the Baptist thought, Matthew 11:3. That is what Peter thought, Matthew 16:21–22. That is what Martha of Bethany thought, John 11:21-27. That is what the apostles thought on the day of Christ's ascension, Acts 1:6. (See Schurer quote, Question 38.) Yes, you know Isaiah 53 speaks of Messiah-Redeemer. How do you know that? The NT revelation tells you, Acts 8:32–35.

No one knew the Messiah-King was to be God incarnate. Mariam was not told. We saw what she was told by Gabriel. Joseph was not told. Yes, the messenger said he would be "God with us Savior," but never in the 700 plus years of the history of interpretation for that passage was the one who would be "God with us" expected to be God incarnate, but God with Israel to bless Israel and rescue the nation Israel from gentile oppression.

The Trinity was not a doctrine revealed in the Old Testament revelation. The evidence is there, but you today understand that evidence because the New Testament revelation told you. The Old Testament belief was "YHWH is one," Deuteronomy 6:4; Zechariah 14:9; Mark 12:29.

The very idea of God in a human body was at that time in history a pagan idea, too similar to the demigods of paganism, or the manifestations of the pagan gods in some common material form.

Let us be rational. Could you have acted normally if you believed your child was God incarnate? Could you have rebuked him, Luke 2:48, as Mariam did? Or thought he was out of his mind, as Mariam and his brothers did, Mark 3:21.

Could you have rebuked him, as Peter did, Matthew 16:21? If you believed Jesus was God, would you have asked him to show you God the Father, as Philip did, John 14:8–9? Would you, a created being, have offered God his own property in exchange for worship, as Satan did, Matthew 4:8–9?

No one—not human beings, not fallen angels—knew Jesus of

Nazareth was deity incarnate. That was by design. God the Son chose to live his mortal life as the incarnate Son of God as a Spirit-filled believer, and he never once stepped out of that role. For thirty-five years, 5 BC to AD 30, he lived a life that was so mundane, so normal, his Nazareth neighbors were offended he was presenting himself as the Messiah-King. All the miraculous works he did during his ministry were believed at the time to be God delegating authority to a prophet, or to the Messiah-King.

Did Jesus occasionally say things that should have led those hearing to believe he was God incarnate? Yes. Matthew 26:64; John 5:17, 23, 26, 40; 14:1, 7–11; 15:26; 17:5 and other clear and unambiguous statements. But they did not believe, because the Holy Spirit did not fructify what they heard, until after his resurrection—and even then "some doubted," Matthew 28:17.

I have a complete discussion of this issue, including a discussion of scriptures that seem to say otherwise, in my book *Biblical Essays IV*, pp. 269–290.

The Roman Catholic Church will show Mariam, and Joseph (see question 32), and shepherds, and Magi worshiping the baby Jesus. That is another Christmas card theology myth.

Mariam knew her son was the coming Messiah-King, but she had not been given the spiritual perception and understanding to know the Messiah-King was God incarnate.

31. Did Joseph know exactly whom his son, Jesus, was?

> Christmas Card Theology seldom mentions Joseph as more than the guy who got Mariam to Bethlehem. What does the Scripture say?

> Answer: Yes … and no.

> Explanation: Mathew 1:21, 23, 25,

>> "She will bear a son, and you will call his name Jesus; for he will save his people from their sins."

>> "Behold, the virgin shall be with child, and bear a son, and they shall call his name 'Immanuel,' which is translated, 'God with us.'"

>> "And did not know her until she had brought forth her firstborn son. And he called his name 'Jesus.'"

> Joseph was told Mariam's child would be a savior and would be God with us. But as I explained in Question 4, the Jews were looking for a Messiah-King to save them from Gentile oppression.

> Joseph, who the same as all others during this period of time was an Old Testament believer without the New Testament revelation (yet to be written), understood "God with us savior" meant God had sent the Messiah to deliver Israel from oppression by the nations. The concept of a coming Messiah-Redeemer to rescue individuals from the penalty due sin was not present at this time in the theology of Israel. (See Schurer quote, Question 38.)

> Yes, the Old Testament revelation testifies of a coming Messiah-Redeemer, e.g., Daniel 9:26; Isaiah 53; Psalm 22, et al. But you know that fact only because the New Testament revelation, e.g., Acts 8:32–35, told you, a revelation the Old Testament believers *did not have*.

> Like Mariam, like many who met or heard of Jesus, Joseph understood his stepson was the Messiah-King to save Israel from Gentile oppression. Joseph did not understand his stepson would be the Redeemer of individuals from sin—that is what the atoning sacrifices of the Law did, e.g., Leviticus 4:35, by grace

through faith. Christ would replace the sacrifices of the Law for sin with the sacrifice of himself for sin. Daniel 9:24, 26; John 1:29; Romans 5:11; 2 Corinthians 5:18–21, but no one of the times knew that. Joseph did not understand Jesus was God incarnate. See Question 30.

32. Did Jesus come to bring peace into the world?

> Christmas Card Theology teaches Jesus was the prince of peace. What does the Scripture say?

Answer: Yes and No.

Explanation: A quick reading of the question may miss that Pastor Hollingsworth carefully said, "peace into the world" not "peace to the world." Yes, Jesus come to bring peace "into the world," Jesus did not come to bring peace to the world.

Jesus brought peace into the world.

> Luke 2:13–14, "And at once there came with the messenger a multitude of the heavenly host, praising God and saying, 14 'Glory in the highest to God, and on earth peace among men of good will.'"
>
> John 15:27, "Peace I [Jesus Christ] leave with you, my peace I give to you; not as the world gives, I give to you. Let not your heart be troubled, nor let it fear."
>
> Romans 5:1, "Therefore, having been justified by faith, we have peace with God through our Lord Jesus Christ."
>
> Philippians 4:7, "the peace of God surpassing all understanding will guard your hearts and your minds in Christ Jesus."
>
> Colossians 3:14, "let the peace of God rule in your hearts, to which also you were called as one body."

Jesus did not come to bring peace to the world.

> Matthew 10:34, "Think not that I came to bring peace to the earth. I came not to bring peace, but a sword."
>
> Luke 12:51–53, "Think you that I came to give peace on the earth? No, I say to you, but rather division. 52 For there will be now five in one house divided, three against two, and two against three. 53 They will be divided father against son and son against father, mother against daughter and daughter against mother, mother-in-law against the daughter-in-law and daughter-in-law against mother-in-law."

Jesus Christ gives individuals peace with God by reconciling the believing sinner to God, and gives the peace of God to all those who have faith in him as the crucified and risen Savior. But to the unbelieving God says, Isaiah 48:22, "There is no peace, saith the Lord, to the ungodly," and Isaiah 57:20–21, "But the unrighteous shall be tossed as troubled waves, and shall not be able to rest. There is no peace to the ungodly, said God."

When Jesus returns as Messiah-King-Redeemer at his second advent, and creates his Davidic-Messianic-Millennial kingdom on the earth, then he will be the Prince of Peace bringing peace to the world through his rule, because he will rule the world with a "rod of iron," Psalm 2:9; Revelation 2:27; 12:5; 19:15.

33. Which gospel does not tell the Christmas story?

> Christmas Card Theology combines the accounts given by Matthew and Luke. What does the Scripture say?
>
> Answer: the Gospel According to Mark does not tell the Christmas story.
>
> Explanation: Matthew 1–2 and Luke 1–2 give the Christmas story. Mark's gospel begins with the ministry of Messiah's herald, John the Baptist, which is about 35 years after John and Jesus were born.
>
> What about John's Gospel? Does John tell the Christmas story? Most will say No. What does the Scripture say?
>
> The Christmas story has many parts, but the core of the story is this, the coming messiah was born into the world. John tells that story.
>
> John 1:10, "He was in the world: and the world came into existence through him; and the world knew him not."
>
> John 1:11, "He came to his own possessions, and his own people did not receive him."
>
> John 1:14, "And the Word became embodied and dwelt among us. And we saw his glory—glory as of a one and only begotten with the Father, full of grace and truth."
>
> [Translation note from the JQTNT. John 1:14, "embodied." The word I have translated "embodied" is *sárx* [Zodhiates, s. v. 4561], living flesh (versus a corpse) or body. The resurgence of the doctrine of Physicalism led to me to make that translation. Physicalism says the deity person God the Son in his incarnation literally stopped being deity and became a human being, though retaining some abilities of deity. Other versions translate "made flesh" (KJV); "became flesh" (YLT, ASV, NKJV, ESV, HCSB, NIV); "became human" (NLT, a translation too much like Physicalism).
>
> [God the Son became embodied in the defined sense of the union of deity with a rational human soul and human body. Deity and human are integral parts of the one person formed by the union. The biblical doctrine is God the Son in his union (the incarnation) with Jesus of Nazareth became one person

with one personality, that of God the Son, with two distinct natures, deity and human, both natures informing the personality, and by that incarnation became the God-man, Jesus the Christ, the Son of God. The Chalcedonian Creed continues to be the orthodox doctrine of the New Testament church. See the Chalcedonian Creed, AD 451, Question 39 and here: https://www.theopedia.com/chalcedonian-creed.]

Above I stated, John the Baptist's ministry began about 35 years after John and Jesus were born. Please allow me to explain.

The dates would be March, 5 BC for John's birth, September, 5 BC for Jesus' birth; the spring of AD 29 for the beginning of John's ministry, and the baptism of Jesus not later than the following February, 29 BC (a new year began in March). The first Passover of Jesus public ministry after his baptism was AD 30, when he announced himself to the Jews.

I have in previous questions (Questions 27, 28) explained the 5 BC birth of John and Jesus. Here I will explain the AD 29 beginning for John's ministry and for Jesus' baptism, and the AD 30 first Passover. The information below is from *God Became Incarnate*, pp. 109–114 (which see for additional discussion).

Luke 3:1 states John began his ministry "in the fifteenth year of the reign of Tiberius Caesar." Some Bible scholars believe Luke is reckoning Tiberius's regnal years from his co-regency with Augustus, beginning AD 11, making the fifteenth year AD 25–26. In this reckoning Jesus died AD 30.

However, neither the Romans nor Tiberius himself used the co-regency method to determine regnal years. There is no manuscript or coin evidence the Romans ever dated regnal years from the beginning of a co-regency.

Tiberius himself reckoned his first regnal year from the death of Augustus, August 19, AD 14, which was the normal Roman method. If one dates the regnal year in the same manner Tiberius dated it, the fifteenth year of his reign was August 19, AD 28 to August 18, AD 29. John began his ministry between those dates. This doesn't mean Jesus was baptized between those dates, but that the Baptist began his ministry at some point between those dates.

Considering that John was baptizing in the Jordan River, the water and weather would be warmer in late spring. Beginning in the spring of the year would give a sufficient period of time before Jesus was baptized to allow John's followers to grow in numbers large enough to attract the attention of the Jewish leaders (John 1:19–28), and prepare the hearts of the people for the messiah. John probably began baptizing in the late spring or early summer of AD 29

To discover when Jesus was baptized by John—a not-later-than date—one must consider the gospel testimony of the number of Passovers in Jesus' ministry. There were four Passovers.

> Passover AD 30, John 2:13
>
> Passover AD 31: Luke 6:1 (cf. Matthew 12:1; Mark 2:23)
>
> Passover AD 32: John 6:4 (cf. Matthew 14:13–21; Mark 6:32–34; Luke 9:10–17)
>
> Passover AD 33, John 19:31 (cf. Matthew 27:50; Mark 16:37; Luke 23:46)

(The Luke 6:1 Passover is based on Leviticus 23:15. See my commentary on Luke's Gospel, vol. 1)

Jesus was baptized before the April 7, AD 30 Passover (fourteen days earlier the year had changed from AD 29 to AD 30). How soon before that Passover? The latest date for Jesus' baptism may be roughly calculated from the events immediately following his baptism, from the Wilderness to the Passover. The minimum number of days was:

Location	Time/Days	Cumulative
Wilderness	5 hours	
Temptation	40 days	40 days
Return to Baptism site	5 hours	41 days
Five disciples	2 days	43 days
To Bethsaida-Galilee	3 days	46 days
To Cana plus Wedding	7.5 days	53.5 days
To Capernaum	7 hours	54 days

Days at Capernaum?   3–14 days?   57–68 days
To Jerusalem/Passover 3–4 days   60–70 days

Working 60–70 days backwards from Passover Nisan 14/April 7, AD 30, and assuming John has included most of the details of Jesus' ministry between the temptation and the Passover, the latest date Jesus could have been baptized was between January 22–February 1, AD 29.

I believe a date between the Feast of Tabernacles in late September in AD 29 and the Feast of Dedication (Hanukkah) in mid-December AD 29 is more likely. Jesus would have attended Tabernacles (a mandatory-attendance Feast), and may have attended Dedication. From one of these Feasts, knowing the time for his public ministry had come, Jesus would have left Jerusalem going east to Jericho and the Jordan River to where John was baptizing.

Jesus was probably baptized after Tabernacles in September AD 29, but certainly no later than February 1, AD 29. He was thirty-four years of age. Three years later, in early April, on the Friday after the AD 33 Passover, Jesus was crucified, died, and was buried. He was thirty-seven years old at his death.

34. Was the announcement to the shepherds by one angel or many angels?

> Christmas Card Theology teaches a choir of angels made the announcement. What does the Scripture say?
>
> Answer: the announcement to the shepherds was made by one of God's messengers.
>
> Explanation: Luke 2:8–12, "And shepherds were in the same region, living in the fields and keeping watch by night over their flock. 9 And a messenger of the Lord stood by them, and the glory of the Lord shone around them, and they greatly feared. 10 And the messenger said to them, 'Do not fear. For behold, I proclaim to you good news, great joy, which will be to all the people. 11 For has been born to you today a savior who is Christ Lord, in David's city. 12 And this to you the sign: you will find a baby, swaddled, and lying in a barn.'"
>
> After the announcement, many messengers appeared to the shepherds and together gave praise to God.
>
> Luke 2:13–14, "And at once there came with the messenger a multitude of the heavenly host, praising God and saying, 14 'Glory in the highest to God, and on earth peace among men of good will.'"
>
> And then all the messengers "went away from them into the heaven," Luke 2:15.

35. What did the angels sing to the shepherds?

> Christmas Card Theology says angels sang praises to God at the announcement of Jesus' birth. What does the Scripture say?
>
> Answer: the Scripture teaches God's messengers (aka: angels) do not sing.
>
> Explanation: Luke 2:13–14, "And at once there came with the messenger a multitude of the heavenly host, praising God and saying, 14 'Glory in the highest to God, and on earth peace among men of good will.'"
>
> In no place in Scripture are God's messengers shown singing. They always "say" not "sing."
>
> The Hebrew text of Job 38:7 reads, "When the morning stars sang together and all the sons of God shouted for joy," when God formed the earth. The "sons of God" who shouted for joy are, in this context, before Adam was created, the created spirit beings known in the Old Testament as *mal'āk*, "messengers." These are the same beings identified by the Greek word *ággelos*, "messengers."
>
> The morning stars who sang together are identified by other scriptures as God the Son, the "bright morning star" (Revelation 22:16) in his pre-incarnate manifestation as the Messenger of YHWH, and the messenger Lucifer, who was holy and sinless at the time because it was before his rebellion against God (Isaiah 14:12–14). Lucifer's body seems to have been created to make music, Ezekiel 28:13, so he made music while God the Son, in his preincarnate manifestation as the Messenger of YHWH (see my book, *Angelology*) sang.
>
> Another example of God's messengers saying not singing is Isaiah 6:1–3 (LXX), "And it came to pass in the year in which king Ozias died, that I saw the Lord sitting on a high and exalted throne, and the house was full of his glory. And seraphs stood round about him: each one had six wings: and with two they covered their face, and with two they covered their feet, and with two they flew. And one cried to the other, and they said, Holy, holy, holy is the Lord of hosts: the whole earth is full of his glory."

Revelation 4:8, "And the four living creatures, they one for one each had six wings encircling and within full of eyes. And they do not have rest day and night, saying, 'Holy, holy, holy the Lord God Almighty, the one having been, and the one being, and the one coming.'"

Revelation 5:11–12, "And I saw, and I heard voices of many messengers encircling the throne, and of the living creatures, and of the elders. And their number was ten thousands of ten thousands and thousands of thousands, 12 saying in a loud voice, 'Worthy is the Lamb having been slain to receive the power, and riches, and wisdom, and strength, and honor, and glory, and blessing.'"

God's messengers are always shown saying not singing. Why God's messengers do not sing is unknown.

36. Where did the shepherds find the newly-born Jesus?

Christmas Card Theology teaches the shepherds find the newly-born Jesus in a little feeding trough filled with hay, surrounded by various animals. Often in Christmas Card Theology the location is a small structure (see any standard "Nativity" scene) in the middle of nowhere. What does the Scripture say?

Answer: The shepherds found the newly-born Jesus in their barn under the Tower of the Flock.

Explanation: Luke 2:15–16, "And it happened, as the messengers went away from them into the heaven, the shepherds kept saying to one another, 'Let us pass through the surrounding area, indeed as far as Bethlehem, and let us see this word that has come, which the Lord declared to us.' 16 And they went quickly and found both Mariam and Joseph, and the baby lying in the barn."

In Question 7, I explained that Jesus was born according to Micah 4:8 at the Tower of the Flock, in the *phátnē*, the stable or barn at the base of the Tower, that the temple shepherds used for birthing lambs or during inclement weather. I explained *phátnē* is the word usually translated "manger," i.e., a feeding trough, and I explained why that translation is wrong. The comparison is between no room for a family in a *katáluma*, versus room for a family in a *phátnē*.

Let us look more closely at the shepherds. (This discussion is drawn from my commentary on Luke's Gospel, vol. 1, lightly edited to the present purpose.)

Now, the shepherds were in the fields that night, because it wasn't too cold and was not raining. As I have shown (Question 28), the date was late August or early September, 5 BC. The average temperature range in modern times for September through October in the Bethlehem area is 63–82 Fahrenheit (17–27 Celsius). Average rainfall is zero. These modern conditions probably approximate environmental conditions in 5 BC. In December, the traditional month, temperatures ranged from 43–57 Fahrenheit (6–13 Celsius), and rainfall was about 3.5 inches (about 9 centimeters).

As the shepherds sat around their campfire, one of God's messengers appeared. The messenger told them to go and find "a Savior, who is the Lord Christ." The messenger said they would, 1) find a baby, 2) wrapped in swaddling cloths, and 3) lying in "the" *phátnē*. In Greek the definite article indicates specific identity. The supposition is that the identity of this particular *phátnē* was known to the shepherds. How could they know which *phátnē*? Well, they had a *phátnē*, their stable under the Tower of the Flock—a stable in which they kept the sheep in inclement weather and birthed lambs. The same place mentioned in Micah 4:8 as the birth place of the Messiah.

After hearing the messenger the shepherds said to one another, "Let us pass through the surrounding area, indeed as far as Bethlehem, and let us see this word that has come, which the Lord declared to us." Most versions have the shepherds saying, "Let us go . . . and see this 'thing.'" The Greek word most versions translate "thing" is *rhḗma* [Zodhiates, s. v. "4487"], "that which is spoken, a statement, word." *Rhḗma* refers to the statement made by the messenger. The Hebrew shepherds left their sheep to find the conditions which fulfilled the prophetic word stated by the messenger.

They went looking for and found "the" specific sign they were told to look for, 2:17, the specific sign which the messenger had given them. What could "the *phátnē*" mean but the stable they knew and used? Is it credible these temple shepherds did not know the prophecy concerning their *phátnē*, Micah 4:8? "They came with haste," so they knew where they were going. Once there they diligently investigated the scene they found to see if it matched the messenger's description.

There, just as the messenger had said, they found the three signs: 1) a baby, 2) wrapped in swaddling cloths, 3) lying in the *phátnē*. After they had seen the baby Jesus they ran to Bethlehem and told everyone who would listen all they had heard from the messenger, and all they had seen in their stable.

Thus Jesus was born at Bethlehem in the *phátnē* under the Tower of the Flock. The Tower of the Flock stands today at the side of the road on the way into Bethlehem. In this stable for birthing lambs the Lamb of God was born.

The church father Jerome (AD 347–420), who lived in Jerusalem, stated the tower was nine-tenths of a mile from Bethlehem [Letter 108, para. 10, Schaff *NPNF*, 6:200; Bromiley, *ISBE*, "Eder, Tower of"). If one searches Google Images for "the tower of the flock," an image of the tower will be displayed. A friend who recently visited Israel said his tour group was shown a tree marking the spot where the tower had been.

37. How old was Jesus when the shepherds came to visit him?

>   Christmas Card Theology teaches the same as Scripture. What does the Scripture say?
>
>   Answer: the scripture does not say Jesus' age when the shepherds found Jesus in their stable. The visit seems to have been soon after he was born, i.e., less than 24 hours after his birth.
>
>   Explanation: Luke 2:7-15, "And she birthed her son, the firstborn, and swaddled him, and laid him in a barn, because there was not a place for them in the lodging.
>
>   8 "And shepherds were in the same region, living in the fields and keeping watch by night over their flock. 9 And a messenger of the Lord stood by them, and the glory of the Lord shone around them, and they greatly feared.
>
>   10 "And the messenger said to them, "Do not fear. For behold, I proclaim to you good news, great joy, which will be to all the people. 11 For has been born to you today a savior who is Christ Lord, in David's city. 12 And this to you the sign: you will find a baby, swaddled, and lying in a barn." 13 And at once there came with the messenger a multitude of the heavenly host, praising God and saying, 14 "Glory in the highest to God, and on earth peace among men of good will.
>
>   15 "And it happened, as the messengers went away from them into the heaven, the shepherds kept saying to one another, "Let us pass through the surrounding area, indeed as far as Bethlehem, and let us see this word that has come, which the Lord declared to us."
>
>   16 "And they went quickly and found both Mariam and Joseph, and the baby lying in the barn."
>
>   The Scripture implies the shepherds saw Jesus shortly after he was born.

38. Did the shepherds know exactly that Jesus was both Savior and Messiah?

> Christmas Card Theology says Jesus is the Savior, but Savior of whom or from what is not part of the message. What does the Scripture say?

> Answer: Yes, the shepherds were told Jesus was both Savior and Messiah.

> Explanation: Luke 2:11, "For has been born to you today a savior who is Christ Lord, in David's city."

The shepherds knew who "Christ" was, because Psalm 2 told them the Christ was the anointed king, 2:2, whose birth was caused by God, Psalm 2:7. In Psalm 2:2 the Hebrew word translated "anointed" is *māshîah*, transliterated "messiah." The Greek equivalent of the Hebrew *māshîah* is *christós*, christ. They knew the one announced by the messenger was the coming Messiah-King. A king is the lord of his subjects, so they knew Jesus was savior, king, Messiah, Christ, and lord, or in the words of the messengers, "Christ Lord."

The shepherds understood, with all other Jews of their times, that the Messiah-King would save Israel gentile oppression. In Question 4 I quoted Historian Emil Schurer, from his work, *A History of the Jewish People in the Time of Jesus Christ*, Division 2, 2:129–130. I will repeat that quotation here.

> "The older Messianic hope virtually moves within the boundary of the then present circumstances of the world, and is nothing else than the hope of a better future for the *nation*. That the nation should be morally purified from all bad elements, that it should exist unmolested and respected in the midst of the Gentile world, whilst its enemies were either destroyed or forced to acknowledge the nation and its God, that it should be governed by a just, wise, and powerful king of the house of David, and that therefore internal justice, peace and happiness would prevail, nay that all natural evils would be abolished and a state of unclouded prosperity would appear—this may be said to have formed the foundation of the future hope

among the older prophets."

That is the person the shepherds understood the baby born in their barn to be: the Messiah-King who would save their nation from gentile oppression.

The translation of Luke 2:11 above gives the words in the same order as the Greek text. The emphasis is the birth of a savior who is the Christ of Psalm 2:2, 7.

The shepherds would have understood the Greek *christós*, "Christ," as their prophesied Messiah. They would also have understood the Greek word *kúrios* (sir, master, lord), in the sense of a king who rules. The Messiah-King was to rule over the gentiles, just as Psalm 2 states. As explained at Question 4, they would not have understood *kúrios*, "Lord," in the sense of God incarnate. That is why we do not see them worshiping. See discussion at Question 4 and my book *Biblical Essays IV*, pp. 269–290.

The fuller and completed New Testament revelation, which the shepherds did not have because not yet written, tells you and me and all others that Jesus the Christ is not only the Messiah-King, but is the Messiah-Redeemer, the Savior of individuals from the penalty due sin. (That same fuller and completed New Testament revelation tells us the Messiah-Redeemer-King is God incarnate.)

Because he is Messiah-Redeemer Jesus suffered on the cross, and died, and was buried, and rose from the grave, to be the Savior of any person who believes in God and God's testimony that the crucified and resurrected Jesus Christ is the Savior of sinners from the penalty due sin. The penalty due sin is spiritual death: separation from God during this mortal life, and, should a sinner die without salvation, the penalty is endless spiritual death and endless punishment in the lake of fire, i.e., hell.

In salvation, God rescues a sinner out of the state of spiritual death and delivers him/her into a permanent state of spiritual life. Salvation is obtained by God's grace through the sinner's faith, not works, and is maintained by God's grace and the limitless merit of Christ's propitiation: his complete satisfaction of God for sin made by his suffering and death on the cross.

In his sufferings and death on the cross, Jesus fully and completely satisfied God for the crime of sin. The limitless merit of that satisfaction is applied to the sinner's spiritual need by God's grace through the means of the sinner's personal faith in God and God's testimony as to the way of salvation.

Repent of your sins and believe on Christ as your Savior, Acts 2:38; 3:19–20; 11:18; Romans 3:22–26; 10:9–10, 13; Galatians 3:22; 1 Peter 1:21; 1 John 3:23.

Because he is Messiah-Kling Jesus is returning to set up his kingdom and rule the world.

39. Did the baby Jesus have a halo?

> Christmas Card Theology teaches the baby Jesus had a halo. The depiction is derived from numerous Renaissance paintings. What does the Scripture say?

Answer: No. The baby Jesus did not have a halo. Neither did Mariam, Joseph, God's messengers, the shepherds, etc. Nobody had a halo.

Explanation: Philippians 2:5–7, "Let this mindset be in you that was also in Christ Jesus, 6 who existing in the essential nature of God, did not regard equality with God for his own advantage, 7 but emptied himself, having taken on his own initiative and power the essential nature of a servant, being in the likeness of men."

A halo, a circle of light surrounding the head, originated in pagan religious beliefs concerning their gods. The ancient Egyptian, Greek, and other gods in the east and far east are depicted with a halo. The symbol is inappropriate to Jesus Christ, any person in Scripture, anyone claiming to be a believer in Jesus Christ—actually no genuine person had or has a halo.

In Philippians 2:5–7, the apostle Paul states God the Son laid aside any outward manifestation of his essential deity in his incarnation. There was no halo. Moreover, although "God is light," 1 John 1:5, and God "dost robe thyself with light as with a garment," Psalm 104:2 (LXX), God does not have a halo.

Philippians 2:5–8 is often misinterpreted to mean God the Son stopped being deity in his incarnation. That is false doctrine. The issue is of great importance. I explain that passage in my commentary on Philippians, pp. 67–72. Here I will state the conclusion of that discussion.

> An expanded translation of Philippians 2:5–8 according the Greek vocabulary and the biblical context would read:
>
> "Let this mindset be in you that was also in Christ Jesus, 6 who existing in the essential nature of God, did not regard equality with God for his own advantage, 7 but emptied himself of all outward manifestation of deity, having taken

on his own initiative and power the essential nature of a servant, being in the likeness of men, sin excepted, 8 and having been found in the physical form of men, he humbled himself, becoming obedient to death, even the death of the cross."

God the Son voluntarily set aside the outward manifestation of deity, and through the exercise of his omnipotent power he made a union of his deity nature and human nature, that he might become human and mortal in order to pay the penalty for the sin of his erring creature man.

At no time did God the Son cease to be deity in his incarnation with Jesus of Nazareth. An incarnation is a union. In a union the things joined together maintain their essential properties. An example. If I join metal with wood to create a hammer, the metal remains exactly as it was prior to the union with the wood, and the wood remains exactly as it was prior to the union with the metal.

In his incarnation, God the Son temporarily set aside only the outward manifestations of his deity. Jesus Christ is God and man, the God-man, one person with one personality, that of God the Son, informed by his two natures, genuine deity and genuine humanity. That is the doctrine of the Scripture and the New Testament church.

The Creed of Chalcedon, AD 451.

> "We, then, following the holy fathers, all with one consent teach men to confess one and the same Son, our Lord Jesus Christ, the same perfect in Godhead and also perfect in manhood; truly God and truly man, of a rational soul and body; coessential with the Father according to the Godhead, and consubstantial with us according to the manhood; in all things like unto us, without sin; begotten before all ages of the Father according to the Godhead, and in these latter days, for us and for our salvation, born of the Virgin Mary, the mother of God, according to the manhood; one and the same Christ, Son, Lord, Only-begotten, to be acknowledged in two natures, without confusion, without change, without division, without

separation; the distinction of natures being by no means taken away by the union, but rather the property of each nature being preserved, and concurring in one person and one subsistence, not parted or divided into two persons, but one and the same Son, and only begotten, God the Word, the Lord Jesus Christ; as the prophets from the beginning have declared concerning Him, and the Lord Jesus Christ Himself has taught us, and the creed of the holy fathers has handed down to us."

The personal subsistence of deity in the Trinity of God that is the person God the Son joined himself to a rational human soul and body by a supra-natural, non-sexual act which procreated a genuine male human being, the person Immanuel-Jesus, in the womb of Mariam, a virgin, in whom Jesus was conceived and from whom he was birthed. Jesus the Christ is one Person with one personality, that of God the Son, a personality informed by his two natures, genuine deity and a genuine rational sinless human soul. He is immaterial deity and immaterial sinless human soul joined in a union animating a genuine material sinless human body, resulting in the sinless person who is both God and man, the God-man.

Every person who has been saved and discipled must submit to these facts in faith and confession.

> Jesus Christ was, is, and always will be God the Son incarnate in Jesus of Nazareth: the God-man.

> Jesus Christ was the God-man at the moment of his incarnation at the conception of Jesus of Nazareth.

> Jesus Christ was the God-man during his life on earth.

> Jesus Christ was the God-man in his sufferings, death, burial, and resurrection.

> Jesus Christ was the God man at his ascension into heaven.

> Jesus Christ is the God-man in the yet future at his second advent, and in his coming Kingdom on earth, and in the new heaven and earth yet to come.

Jesus Christ was, is, and endlessly will be the God-man: God the Son incarnate in Jesus of Nazareth.

(Note: not a halo on the cover it is the light from the lamp.)

40. Who were the first recorded human witnesses for Christ?

>Christmas Card Theology teaches nothing about a witness for Christ. What does the Scripture say?
>
>Answer: shepherds keeping watch by night over their flock.
>
>Explanation: Luke 2:15–18, "And it happened, as the messengers went away from them into the heaven, the shepherds kept saying to one another, 'Let us pass through the surrounding area, indeed as far as Bethlehem, and let us see this word that has come, which the Lord declared to us.'
>
>16 "And they went quickly and found both Mariam and Joseph, and the baby lying in the barn. 17 Then seeing, they proclaimed concerning the saying that was told them concerning this child. 18 And all those hearing marveled concerning the things spoken to them by the shepherds."
>
>That the shepherds "went quickly and found both Mariam and Joseph, and the baby lying in the barn" suggests they knew where they were going. The only barn relevant to these particular shepherds was their barn. At the least we may say they went first to their barn.
>
>In their barn, the shepherds saw the three things the messenger had said to them to properly identify the one born as "savior who is Christ Lord, in David's city." Those three things were 1) a baby; 2) a baby swaddled; 3) a baby swaddled lying in a barn.
>
>The word "swaddled" may be unfamiliar to readers. The word means wrapped in cloths. Every newborn was swaddled. The ancient Jewish practice of swaddling involved specific actions. After the umbilical cord was cut and tied, the baby was sprinkled with powder made of dried myrtle leaves. Then a small amount of finely ground salt was applied to the skin. The baby would then be wrapped in a square yard of cloth, with arms along the body and legs stretched out, from shoulders to ankles. The practice had physical and spiritual meaning for the parents. From [chaimbentorah.com. Article: *Hebrew Word Study: Swaddling Clothes.*]

Because every newborn was swaddled, the key sign of the three signs to the shepherds was a newborn lying in a barn. This also suggests the shepherds knew which barn the messenger intended. Micah 4:8 spoke of their barn. Naturally their barn would be the one they first visited, and finding the baby, they stopped looking.

After seeing the child, the shepherds "proclaimed concerning the saying that was told them concerning this child. And all those hearing marveled concerning the things spoken to them by the shepherds." Although Luke's account implies the shepherds went out into the night and woke people from sleep, nothing so discourteous need be imagined. We need to ask and answer three questions.

Question 1. Where did the shepherds testify? Bethlehem was less than a mile south of the Tower. The shepherds most likely lived in Bethlehem. God's messenger had told the shepherds "Christ Lord" had been born "in David's city" (in Question 7 I noted the Tower was in the suburbs of Bethlehem, or in the words of the shepherds, Luke 2:15, the area surrounding Bethlehem). Therefore it is natural the shepherds testified in David's city, Bethlehem.

Question 2. When did the shepherds testify? Many defer to the hymn, "It Came Upon a Midnight Clear," assuming Jesus was born about midnight and shortly after the shepherds saw him and went testifying in the darkness of the early morning hours. However, the Scripture does not say, and therefore we are to use our powers of common sense and deductive reasoning.

First, let me address the hymn, "It Came Upon a Midnight Clear." This hymn was written in 1849 by Edmund Sears, pastor of a Unitarian Church. Mr. Sears grew tired of his congregation singing about Christ, the incarnation, and the nativity. So he wrote a song that reduced Christ to a nameless "it," and focused on incidentals in the Christmas story.

The Scripture does not say the hour Christ was born. God's messengers appeared to the shepherds as they were "keeping watch by night over their flock." The sun may have just set; the sun may have been below the horizon in the twilight before dawn; or any time between.

Let us be reasonable. Coming to homes and banging on doors where the lights are off and all are in bed would not have been a good time to testify David's heir, the Christ Lord, has been born in their barn. The shepherds' testimony was in the early evening or after the breaking dawn.

Question 3. To whom did the shepherds testify? Most likely to their immediate and extended families. If their testimony extended over several days, then to all who would hear.

There is always an appropriate manner, time, and place for proclaiming the Good News. The shepherds did not go around after midnight banging on every door in Bethlehem. So we also should be willing to respond to those appropriate times and places where and when the Holy Spirit provides opportunities to proclaim the Good News.

41. Was shepherding considered a very noble profession?

> Christmas Card Theology says nothing about the shepherds, except noting they exist. What does the Scripture say?

> Answer: No.

> Explanation: Shepherding was considered ritually unclean according to the religious laws of the times. Everybody ate sheep, but few wanted to be a shepherd.

42. What was Jesus' first recorded journey?

> Christmas Card Theology leaves Jesus in the barn where he was born. What does the Scripture say?

Answer: Jesus' first recorded journey was to the temple in Jerusalem, forty-one days after his birth.

Explanation: Luke 2:22, "And when the days of their purification were fulfilled according to the Law of Moses, they brought him to Jerusalem, to present him to the Lord, 23 as it is written in the Law of the Lord: every male opening a womb shall be called holy to the Lord, 24 and offer a sacrifice, according to that declared in the Law of the Lord, a pair of doves or two young pigeons."

Jesus' first recorded journey was not for his circumcision, Luke 2:21. Circumcision could be performed anywhere, in the home if not in the temple, on the eighth day of his birth.

There are three commands of YHWH affecting Jesus' first recorded journey.

> Deuteronomy 12:5–7 (LXX), "But in the place which the Lord thy God shall choose in one of your cities to name his name there, and to be called upon, ye shall even seek him out and go thither. And ye shall carry thither your whole-burnt-offerings, and your sacrifices, and your first-fruits, and your vowed-offerings, and your freewill-offerings, and your offerings of thanksgiving, the first-born of your herds, and of your flocks. And ye shall eat there before the Lord your God, and ye shall rejoice in all the things on which ye shall lay your hand, ye and your houses, as the Lord your God has blessed you."

> That place for Joseph, Mariam, and Jesus was Jerusalem. King David brought the Ark of the Covenant into Jerusalem ca. 1000 BC, about 400 years after Israel entered the promised land (under Joshua, ca. 1400 BC) and David set up the tent of meeting around the Ark as per YHWH's instruction to Moses in Exodus 26. (David's son Solomon built the temple.)

Leviticus 12:2–4 (LXX), "Speak to the children of Israel, and thou shalt say to them, Whatsoever woman shall have conceived and born a male child shall be unclean seven days, she shall be unclean according to the days of separation for her monthly courses. And on the eighth day she shall circumcise the flesh of his foreskin. And for thirty-three days she shall continue in her unclean blood; she shall touch nothing holy, and shall not enter the sanctuary, until the days of her purification be fulfilled."

The thirty-three days began their countdown to purification on the day after circumcision on the eighth day [Chill, 184].

Leviticus 12:6–8 (LXX), "And when the days of her purification shall have been fulfilled for a son or a daughter, she shall bring a lamb of a year old without blemish for a whole-burnt-offering, and a young pigeon or turtle-dove for a sin-offering to the door of the tabernacle of witness, to the priest. And he shall present it before the Lord, and the priest shall make atonement for her, and shall purge her from the fountain of her blood; this is the law of her who bears a male or a female. And if she cannot afford a lamb, then shall she take two turtle-doves or two young pigeons, one for a whole-burnt-offering, and one for a sin-offering; and the priest shall make atonement for her, and she shall be purified."

Miriam offered "according to that declared in the Law of the Lord, a pair of doves or two young pigeons," Luke 2:24. They were very poor, too poor to afford a lamb. The cost of a sheep in the 1st century AD is unknown. Today a young sheep costs about $200.00–250.00. Taking the lower value and dividing by a day's wage of $7.25/hour equals about 27 day's wages. In the first century, a day's wage was ten to twelve *assárion* (a *denarius* was sixteen assárion.) Using the lower figure, a young sheep cost about nineteen *denarii*, or about seven *shekels*, which was about twenty-five days' wages. Too much for Joseph and Mariam.

43. Who recognized Jesus as Messiah, and blessed him, during Jesus' first recorded journey?

> Christmas Card Theology does not say, because it leaves Jesus in the barn where he was born. What does the Scripture say?
>
> Answer: a man named Simeon recognized Jesus as Messiah, and blessed him.
>
> Explanation: Luke 2:25–35, "And behold, there was a man in Jerusalem whose name was Simeon. And this man was righteous and devout, waiting for the Consolation of Israel, and the Holy Spirit was upon him. 26 And it was divinely revealed to him by the Holy Spirit not to see death before he might see the Lord's Christ. 27 And he came, by the Spirit, into the temple, and when the parents were bringing in the child Jesus, they to do for him according to that custom of the Law.
>
> 28 "Then Simeon received him into his arms, and blessed God, and said, 29 'Now you are letting your servant depart, Lord, according to your word, in peace. 30 For my eyes have seen your deliverance, 31 which you prepared before the face of all the peoples, 32 a light for revelation to the gentiles and glory of your people Israel.'
>
> 33 "And his father and mother were marveling at the things having been spoken concerning him. 34 And Simeon blessed them, and said to Mariam his mother, 'Consider this, he is appointed for the falling and rising of many in Israel, and for a sign spoken against, 35 and of you also a sword will go through your soul, so that the thoughts of many hearts may be revealed.'"

Perhaps the most amazing thing about this testimony is not that Simeon was promised he would not die "before he might see the Lord's Christ." It is not that the Holy Spirit brought Simeon "into the temple … when the parents were bringing in the child Jesus."

The most amazing thing is this important testimony was for Joseph and Mariam alone. They needed the reminder their son was the Messiah-King who would deliver his nation Israel from their enemies. They "were marveling at the things" Simeon said, because everything concerning their life with Jesus was so normal, so mundane, that it was easy for them to forget Jesus was "Son of the Most High" and "the Lord God will give him the throne of David, his father" and "he will reign over the house of Jacob to the ages," and "of his kingdom there will not be an end."

Yet their life with Jesus was so normal, so utterly human in every aspect of family life, that she could rebuke him, Luke 2:48, as she would any other child. She sought to raise him to be the messiah God meant him to be, not knowing he was her God and Savior.

Do we not also hear Simeon as we read the Christmas story in Luke's gospel? This is what the reader of the four gospels must understand. Jesus showed us how to live a life of faith as Holy Spirit filled believers. Jesus the Christ, the God-man, chose to live his life among us as a fully human life, not depending on his omnipotence or omniscience as God, but living as a Holy Spirit-filled man of faith, just as his saved people must live their life, in submission to and dependence upon God. His miracles were works to point sinners the Father, even as we today point to the miracles recorded in the gospels to direct sinners to the Savior.

44. Who is the second recorded human witness for Christ, during Jesus' first recorded journey?

> Christmas Card Theology does not say, because it leaves Jesus in the barn where he was born. What does the Scripture say?

Answer: A woman named Anna recognized Jesus as Messiah, and testified about him.

Explanation: Luke 2:36–38, "And there was Anna, a prophetess, daughter of Phanuel of the tribe of Asher. She was much advanced in years, having lived with a husband seven years from her marriage, 37 and she a widow, of about eighty-four years, who did not leave the temple, with fastings and prayers serving night and day. 38 And she at that hour, standing nearby, praising God, and was speaking concerning him to all those waiting for the deliverance of Israel."

Anna also praised the Jesus, perhaps hearing Simeon, or perhaps directly informed by the Holy Spirit. She spoke of him to others. The Holy Spirit does not tell us the content of Anna's "praising God," but she was "speaking concerning him to all those waiting for the deliverance of Israel." The Holy Spirit does not tell the reader the effect of her witness to others.

As students of the Word of God, we are able to understand praising God. Praise to God is vocal applause that declares appreciation of God's person, character, and works. To praise God is to acclaim him for who he is and give thanks for what he has done.

What had God done? Luke tells us through Anna's praise. God had sent the Christ "to all those waiting for the deliverance of Israel." The "deliverance of Israel" was the work of the Messiah-King rescuing the nation from gentile oppression, Psalm 2. See also Question 4, the quote from Schurer in his *History of the Jewish People in the Time of Jesus Christ*. Compare Mariam at Luke 1:51–53.

The biblical Christmas story focuses on Messiah-King as redeemer of the nation from gentile oppression. That was the messianic expectation of the times. Read the four gospels for the whole story of the Messiah-Redeemer-King.

45. Where did Jesus and his family live immediately after he was presented in Jerusalem?

>Christmas Card Theology leaves Jesus and family in the barn. What does the Scripture say?
>
>Answer: Joseph's family returned to their house in Bethlehem immediately after Jesus was presented in Jerusalem.
>
>Explanation: Matthew 2:11, "And having come into the house, they [the wise men] looked at the child with Mariam his mother."

We know from Scripture the family was in a house when the wise men visited. Therefore it is reasonable the family was in living in a house in Bethlehem when they presented Jesus in the temple. His presentation in the temple was on the forty-first day after his birth.

Matthew 2:11, 13, 19–23 seem to conflict with Luke 2:39, "And when they had completed all according to the Law of the Lord, they returned to Galilee, to their town Nazareth." We should accept that leaving out information does not create a contradiction. As does every author, even the human authors of inspired Scripture, each man wrote that which fit his purpose in writing, according to the guidance each received from the Holy Spirit, so that what each wrote was what God wanted written.

Luke jumps from the presentation in the temple to the move to Nazareth. Luke leaves out Matthew's bit about the wise men, the flight to Egypt, and the return to Nazareth. He undoubtedly knew what Matthew had written, but neither Luke nor the Holy Spirit thought what Matthew had written about those things was relevant to Luke's account. If Matthew's purpose was a gospel to evangelize the Jews, and Luke's purpose was a gospel to evangelize gentiles, then what each said, or did not say, fits those purposes.

The story of the wise men is told in Matthew 2:1–12. Because Questions 46–52 focus on the wise men. I will reserve further explanation for those questions.

When did Joseph move his family into a house in Bethlehem? The Scripture does not say. However, we may reason from common experience and common sense.

The time between Jesus' birth and his presentation in the temple was forty-one days. Let us suppose Jesus was born September 1, 5 BC. Forty-one days later was October 11, 5 BC. In October in the year 5 BC the following Feasts took place on the dates indicated.

October 2, 5 BC. Feast of Trumpets

October 11, 5 BC, Day of Atonement

October 16–22, Feast of Tabernacles

Tabernacles was one of the three mandatory attendance Feasts (Exodus 23:14–16), meaning all adult males in Israel must attend the Feast of Tabernacles.

Using September 1 as the day of Jesus birth, then on September 8, 5 BC Jesus was circumcised. On October 11, 5 BC Jesus was presented in the temple, where Simeon and Anna saw him.

Common sense tells us Joseph and family did not stay for very long in the shepherds' barn at the Tower of the Flock. At the most they stayed a few days. Common experience tells every parent reading this account that Jospeh and Mariam sought other living arrangements. The visiting population of Bethlehem had swollen for the census, but that same visiting population was in constant flux as people came and went to be counted in the census.

Therefore, both common sense and common experience tell us Joseph was able to find either (1) an available guest room (*kataluma*) to get the family out the barn while he looked for a house, or (2) he found a house available to rent. Remember, Question 21, Joseph and family used the census as one reason to make a permanent household move to Bethlehem. A person with a house to rent would rather rent to someone permanent than someone in-and-out of town for the census.

Therefore it is likely Joseph and Mariam and Jesus moved into a house before his circumcision, and certainly before his presentation in the temple. Although no one is able to say with certainty, it seems most reasonable that the family was living in a house in Bethlehem long before Mariam's forty-one days of purification had expired. After Jesus' presentation in the temple, the family returned to the house they were renting in Bethlehem.

46. Of the wise men who visited Jesus and his family, how many were there, and what were their names?

> Christmas Card Theology teaches three wise men and names them Melchior, Caspar, and Balthasar. What does the Scripture say?
>
> Answer: Neither the names nor the numbers of the wise men are known.
>
> Explanation: There is no scripture explanation, because there is no scripture revealing names or numbers. Matthew 2:11 states three gifts the wise men gave in honor of the newly born king (Matthew 2:2), so Christmas Card Theology oversimplifies and supposes three wise men giving one gift each. (That reasoning is as valid as Larson's cartoon of a fourth wise man turned away because he brought fruitcake.)
>
> What does the Scripture state, and what may be reasonably concluded from the Scripture? The Scripture says, Matthew 2:3, "But having heard [what the wise men had said about a king], Herod the king was troubled, and all Jerusalem with him."
>
> For all Jerusalem to be troubled supposes more than three travelers. Jerusalem was a major city, and a waypoint for commerce. Three men on camels would not have aroused curiosity, let alone trouble. A large caravan asking for the newly born King of the Jews would.
>
> Considering the travel realities of the day—everyone travelled by foot, important people traveled with a large caravan to discourage robbers—more than three wise men had traveled in a caravan probably numbering fifty or more people, plus camels, with donkeys hauling carts with all the necessities for a long period of travel overland. Preparation time for a large caravan and a long journey would be two to three months. Although some cities, e.g., Jericho, had a *pandocheíon* (think of a hostel or a Motel Six), or a *katáluma* [an enclosed area with niches in the walls for people and animals, see Question 7], most nights while travelling would have been spent by the side of the road in a tent.
>
> [Note, a *pandocheíon* was similar to a modern hostel. When the

Good Samaritan left the injured man in Jericho, he left him at the *pandocheíon* in the care of the manager. The word *pandocheíon* translates to "khan," a trading center and hostel in the ancient Middle East, N. Africa, and Central Asia.]

47. Were the wise men kings, as in the carol, "We Three Kings of Orient are?"

> Christmas Card Theology teaches the three wise men were kings, or gives that impression by the way they are dressed in various drawings, paintings, or nativity scenes. What does the Scripture say?

Answer: No the wise men who visited the baby Jesus were not kings, they were magi.

Explanation: Matthew 2:1, "Now Jesus, having been born in Bethlehem of Judea in the times of Herod the king, behold, wise men [*mágos*] from the east arrived at Jerusalem."

The reason the JQTNT translates the Greek *mágos* in Matthew 2:1 as "wise men," is because that was their function in their society. They were the astronomers, scientists, astrologists, dream interpreters, and political consultants in their culture, serving as advisors to kings.

From ancient times, king and pharaohs and other rulers had as advisors men who watched the skies, interpreted the signs, and maintained the scientific knowledge of the day. They interpreted astronomical signs and the dreams of kings with a view to political and religious events. Those were the *mágos* who came to pay Jesus homage.

One of the questions Christmas Card Theology never asks, and therefore never answers, is why wise men came from a foreign land to Israel to see Jesus. Matthew 2:2 says the wise men asked, "Where is the one who was born King of the Jews? For we saw his star in the east and have come to do homage to him."

They came based on an astronomical sighting (see Question 49) observed while they were in their own country (see Question 48). They came based on an ancient prophecy given by one of their own, the prophet Balaam, ca. 1444–1406 BC, during Israel's forty years of wilderness wanderings.

> Numbers 24:17–19 (LXX), I will point to him, but not now; I bless him, but he draws not near: a star shall rise out of

Jacob, a man shall spring out of Israel; and shall crush the princes of Moab, and shall spoil all the sons of Seth. And Edom shall be an inheritance, and Esau his enemy shall be an inheritance of Israel, and Israel wrought valiantly. And one shall arise out of Jacob, and destroy out of the city him that escapes.

In 5 BC, the wise men saw the star, standing over the place they recognized as the ancient nation Israel. Because this was a prophecy from a pagan prophet, Balaam, it is not unlikely the prophecy was filed in their astronomy-astrology-divination library under "Israel, star."

Most students of the Bible only pay attention to 24:17. The full prophecy, through 24:19, foretells the destruction of certain nations: Moab, Sheth, Edom, and Seir. These nations were descendants of Esau, Genesis 36; Deuteronomy 2; 1 Chronicles 1; who lived in the Arabic countries to the east and south of Israel.

Why did these *mágos* know this ancient prophecy? Why would an ancient prophecy be maintained for ca. 1400 years? The most reasonable answer is the pagan prophet Balaam lived in of the same region as the *mágos*.

Having seen the star, and having consulted their library, the *mágos* came to Jerusalem to pay homage to the newly born king. The Greek word the JQTNT translates as "homage" is *proskunéō*, "to worship, do obeisance, show respect, fall or prostrate before ... literally to throw a kiss in token of respect or homage" [Zodhiates, s. v. 4352].

Literally the wise men (*mágos*) said "we have come to bow to him," but culturally they had come to recognize him as a king. They had had not come to worship in the sense Christians think of worship toward Jesus Christ, which is why I have translated the word "to do homage to."

Certain "wise men" from the East, not kings but *mágos*, met with Herod in their search for one born "King of the Jews," a search based on an astronomical sighting while they were still in their own country.

48. Where were the Magi from?

Christmas Card Theology does not actually say where the *mágos* came from. In Christmas Card Theology the *mágos* somehow arrive on camels, or on foot, at the structure where Jesus lies in a feeding trough. What does the Scripture say?

Answer: The *mágos* were from the east.

Explanation: Matthew 2:1, "Now Jesus, having been born in Bethlehem of Judea in the days of Herod the king, behold, wise men from the east arrived at Jerusalem."

Most Bible scholars think by "from the east" Matthew means Babylon (modern southern Iraq) or Parthia (modern Iran). However, that is not what Matthew meant. There are four lines of evidence in the Scripture pointing to a location other than Babylon or Parthia.

The first line of evidence is Balaam's prophecy (see Questions 47, 49) that foretold the destruction of certain nations: Moab, Sheth, Edom, and Seir. These nations were descendants of Esau, Genesis 36; Deuteronomy 2; 1 Chronicles 1; who lived in the Arabic countries to the south of Israel. The *mágos* in those countries had a natural interest in Balaam's prophecy.

The second line of evidence is the prophet Balaam lived in the region of Moab, Sheth, Edom, and Seir, which is why his prophecy was maintained in the archives of the *mágos* of the region.

The person thinking that "from the east" must mean the area of ancient Babylon or Parthia must answer how those *mágos* obtained a prophecy given 500 miles to the east, and why they would maintain a prophecy for 1,400 years that had nothing to do with Babylon or Parthia. In 1400 BC Babylon was a small city that had been under the control of the Hittites for 200 years, and the Parthian Empire (247 BC–AD 224) did not exist. Jacob was a man who died ca. 1650 BC, the patriarch of the people Israel, who had been wandering in the desert for almost forty years. No one in Babylonia knew, or would have cared if they knew.

The third line of evidence is how the Scripture uses geographical terms, i.e., how Israel in Old Testament times understood geographical terms in relation to the nations.

The country to the south was Egypt. Literally, the country we know today as Saudi Arabia is directly south of Israel and Egypt is to the southwest. But Egypt is always spoken of as from the south because when the military forces of Egypt attacked Israel—as happened many times—those forces entered Israel at the southern end of the nation. The Arabic countries, which were geographically to the south and southeast, such as Moab, Sheth, Edom, and Seir, attacked from the east, across the Jordan River crossing at Jericho.

What about countries directly to the east, what we think of as southern Iraq and Iran? Israel knew that region as the Babylonian and Medo-Persian Empires. Scripture describes those countries as from the north.

When Gentiles living in the regions today known as Iraq and Iran attacked Israel, they followed the "Fertile Crescent" formed by the Tigris and Euphrates Rivers, which caused them to attack from the north. No army could cross the 725 KM (450 mi.) of desert between Israel and Babylonia. They followed the Fertile Crescent north from their cities, and then east into Syria, and then south into Israel and Egypt. From Israel's perspective, the Babylonians and Persians attacked from the north, so Scripture identifies them as from the north.

From the east means modern-day Jordan and Saudi Arabia, because the Arabic traders entered Israel by crossing the Jordan River near Jericho. The *mágos* who came looking for the "King of the Jews" were Arabians from what the Old Testament peoples named Ammon, Moab, Seir (Edom), and Midian; in modern terms, Jordan (Ammon, Moab, Seir/Edom) and Saudi Arabia (Midian). They came into Jerusalem from the east.

The fourth line of evidence the *mágos* were from the countries of Balaam's prophecy is the three gifts mentioned in Matthew 2:11, gold, frankincense, and myrrh. Their gifts are appropriate to an Arabian origin.

There is a fifth line of evidence. The *mágos* left Bethlehem by a southern route leading to Arabia, Matthew 2:12. The road south from Jerusalem to Bethlehem continued through Bethlehem then continued south into Arabia.

Why did they not use that road when they went to Jerusalem? Because the major trade road, known as the King's Highway, went north from Arabia, past the east side of the Dead Sea, to the Jericho Crossing of the Jordan River, and from there into Jericho, where there was a *pandocheíon* (see Question 46), and then the main trade road leading up the mountain into Jerusalem. Jerusalem was the capitol of ancient Israel, and currently the capitol of Herod's Kingdom, so what better place to look for a king?

49. Did the wise men follow the star from the east?

> Christmas Card Theology teaches a star announcing Jesus' birth, but is less clear as to what the star had to do with the wise men appearing at the barn. What does the Scripture say?
>
> Answer: No, the wise men did not follow the star from the east.
>
> Explanation: Matthew 2:2, "saying, 'Where is the one who was born King of the Jews? For we saw his star in the east and have come to do homage to him.'"
>
> Considering the travel realities of the day—everyone travelled by foot, and important people with a large caravan—the wise men coming from Arabia (see Question 48) could not have made a trip from their homeland with less than two or three months preparation and travel time.
>
> I discussed above (see Question 48) four reasons the wise men were most likely from Arabia, i.e., from the nations listed in Balaam's prophecy (Question 47), including Midian (modern Saudi Arabia). They entered Israel from the east at the Jordan Crossing a few miles east of Jericho.
>
> Interpreters of Matthew 2:2 make the assumption that "we saw his star in the east" means the wise men were living in the east, in Babylonia or Parthia, and from that perspective saw the star in the western sky. But wise men may have meant they saw the star in the eastern sky. From the perspective of the countries south (Midian) and southeast (e.g., Moab) of Israel, the star would have been northerly in the eastern sky, which is to say far from the setting sun in the west.
>
> The wise men said the "saw" the star and came to Israel, they did not say they "followed" the star and came to Israel. The star appeared for a little while, then disappeared. The wise men followed Balaam's prophecy, "a star shall rise out of Jacob, a man shall spring out of Israel," Numbers 24:17 (LXX). Of course, the wise men from countries south and southwest of Israel thought of Israel as in the east, because they entered Israel from the east at the Jericho crossing.
>
> The star seen, not seen, then seen again is supported by

Matthew 2:9–10, "Now, having heard the king, they went. And they saw the star—the one they saw in the east—going before them until it came and stood over where the child was. 10 Now when they had seen the star they earnestly rejoiced with great joy."

The "star" was not an astronomical phenomenon. This sign of the messiah's birth first appeared in the sky in a position relative to the location of the wise men that made it seem to be over the land of Jacob/Israel. Then the star disappeared. After the wise men visited Herod the star reappeared and led them to the house where Jesus was living—it moved and then it stopped over the house.

A genuine star is fixed in the heavens. The stars only seem to move as the earth rotates on its axis from night to day. The apparent movement of the stars as the earth rotates is east to west. The sign of messiah's birth moved south and then stopped. From Jerusalem to Bethlehem was in those days about five miles, about an hour and one-half walk. A genuine star would not have seemed to move over that distance during that period of time.

Some believe the star was a comet, which appeared in the sky, then disappeared as it went behind the sun, then reappeared just in time to guide the wise men to the house. But comets don't stop and hover over a house. Chinese astronomers saw a supernova for 70 days in 5/4 BC, which some identify as a comet, thus accounting for it appearing, disappearing (behind the sun), and then reappearing. There was a conjunction of Saturn and Jupiter in 7 BC and in 6 BC Mars joined this conjunction. Haley's comet appeared in 12/11 BC, but this is too early.

If the phenomenon the wise men saw was a normal phenomenon, it would have remained in the same relative position, and stop when they stopped. But the phenomenon moved on its own, and it stopped on its own, and it distinctly located itself over the house. Not high in the sky as a star, but low over one specific house.

Might not the original sighting correspond with Luke 2:13, the multitude of the heavenly host praising God at the birth of Jesus? And the next sighting one or more of that heavenly host, messengers of God, guiding the wise men to Jesus? Regardless, "his star in the east" was a supernatural event, not the astronomical phenomenon Christmas Card Theology makes it to be, or the wise men thought it to be.

50. When Herod heard about Jesus, was he the only one troubled by the news?

> Christmas Card Theology seldom mentions Herod, or anyone in Jerusalem. What does the Scripture say?

Answer: No.

Explanation: Matthew 2:1–3, "Now Jesus, having been born in Bethlehem of Judea in the times of Herod the king, behold, wise men from the east arrived at Jerusalem, 2 saying, "Where is the one who was born King of the Jews? For we saw his star in the east and have come to do homage to him." 3 But having heard, Herod the king was troubled, and all Jerusalem with him."

Herod was troubled because the birth of "the one who was born King of the Jews" was a threat to his rule. Herod killed anyone who seemed to be a threat to his rule, including members of his family. Those in Jerusalem were troubled because Herod was troubled.

Herod was such an evil man that he had given an order to his sister Salome, that when he died she was to have "all the principle men of the entire Jewish nation" (whom, as he lay dying, he had ordered to be gathered in the hippodrome in Jerusalem) to be executed so there would be mourning; which she did not do [Josephus, *Antiquities*, 17.6.5].

51. Did the wise men visit Jesus in the stable?

> Christmas Card Theology leaves Jesus in the barn where he was born. What does the Scripture say?
>
> Answer: the wise men visited Jesus in a house.
>
> Explanation: Matthw 2:9, 11, "Now, having heard the heard the king, they went. And they saw the star—the one they saw in the east—going before them until it came and stood over where the child was …. And having come into the house, they looked at the child with Mariam his mother. And falling down they did homage to him. And opening their riches, they brought gifts to him: gold and frankincense and myrrh."
>
> At Question 45 I discussed Joseph moving his family into a house in Bethlehem. In Question 49 I discussed the "star" moving ahead of the wise men as the left Jerusalem and stopping over a house.
>
> The current question provides an opportunity to discuss the usefulness of the gifts. When Herod realized the wise men were not returning to tell him where they had found "the one who was born King of the Jews" (they having been warned by God in a dream not to return to Herod, Matthew 2:13), Herod decided to kill all the children two years of age and under in the region of Bethlehem, "according to the time which he had inquired from the wise men," i.e., when they had first seen the star.
>
> After the wise men left Bethlehem, a "messenger of the Lord appears in a dream to Joseph, saying, 'Get up. Take the child and his mother and escape to Egypt, and remain there until I may tell you; for Herod is about to look for the child to destroy him,'" Matthew 2:14.
>
> Now Joseph and Mariam had recently made a big move from Nazareth to Bethlehem, to make a new home and start a new business in Bethlehem. How did they fund a bigger move to Egypt so soon after moving to Bethlehem?
>
> They had been living in Bethlehem for several months, perhaps longer. We know from historical events that Herod died

between March 12 and April 11, 4 BC. Josephus reports that shortly before Herod's death there was an eclipse of the moon. It is the only eclipse mentioned by Josephus and occurred March 12/13, 4 BC. The Passover was celebrated after Herod's death on April 11, 4 BC. Therefore Herod died between March 12 and April 11, 4 BC.

We also know Herod reigned for 34 years. The 34th year of his reign began March 29, 4 BC, so his death occurred sometime between March 29 and April 11, 4 BC.

The meeting with the wise men had to occur early enough before his death for all the subsequent events to take place: Herod meeting with the wise men; Herod waiting for their return; Herod's murder of the infants; the eclipse; Herod's 34th year as King began; Herod's death before the Passover.

As noted above, a two to three month preparation and journey for a large caravan would be normal to the times; perhaps longer. Herod sent soldiers to murder all the male children that were in Bethlehem and surrounding region, from two years old and under, according to the time which he had inquired from the wise men.

I have defended a September, 5 BC birth for Jesus (Question 28 and my book *God Became Incarnate*). Herod died a few days after 5 BC became 4 BC, which occurred on March 28. Assuming the star appeared on the day of Jesus' birth in September 5 BC, it was about seven months before Herod died, and the wise men saw Herod about three months after the birth (if the estimate of preparation and travel time is correct, see Question 46).

The date when the star appeared in relation to Jesus' birth is not certain because the Scripture does not say. Herod may have had children two years old and under killed out of an abundance of caution. However, God might have shown the wise men the star two years before a 5 BC birth to ensure they arrived at the right time—a September 6 BC or a 7 BC birth is also possible.

Regardless of the timing of the star, Joseph needed to fund a move of his family, their household goods, and his work tools from Bethlehem to Egypt. From Bethlehem to the Egyptian border, which is to say the Sinai Peninsula, is about forty miles. But if we are speaking of moving to Alexandria, Egypt, where there was a large colony of Jews, the distance is about 300 miles, or about three times the distance between Nazareth and Bethlehem.

How did Joseph fund the move? "And opening their [the wise men's] riches, they brought gifts to him: gold and frankincense and myrrh." God is an on time practical God who supplies for our needs. Gold supplied the immediate need for funding the move. Frankincense and myrrh were used for expensive perfumes, and so could be sold to fund later needs. Joseph would have set some of money aside for the return trip.

One final comment. Modern social justice warriors like to speak of Joseph and family as Palestinian refugees fleeing injustice. No, Jesus was not a political refugee. God directed the move and the return. Jesus and family never left the Roman Empire (the move to Egypt from Judea was like moving from one state to another in the same country).The family was not persecuted, they were threatened by a local ruler.

Moreover, the move was self-funded (the gifts from the wise men), and the family took all their possessions with them to begin a new life, in a new home, and continuing employment in the place God had told them to live until God called them to return.

God's purpose in the move was not only to preserve their lives, but also as fulfillment of messianic prophecy. Matthew 2:15, "that might be fulfilled that spoken by the Lord through the prophet [Hosea 11:1], saying, 'Out of Egypt I have called my son.'"

Joseph and family were in no sense like the political refugees of modern times.

52. How old was Jesus when the wise men saw him?

> Christmas Card Theology teaches the wise men saw Jesus on the day he was born, because it shows shepherds and wise men together. What does the Scripture say?
>
> Answer: The Scripture does not state Jesus' age when he was seen by the wise men.
>
> Explanation: Matthew 2:16, "Then Herod, when he understood that he had been deceived by the wise men, was very angry, and he sent to put to death all the male children that were in Bethlehem and in all its region, from two years old and under, according to the time which he had inquired from the wise men."
>
> What we do know is Jesus was living in a house when the wise men saw him. Based on the time of Herod's death, and estimated preparation and travel time for the wise men after seeing the star "in the east," Jesus was at least several months old when the wise men saw him.

53. Did Jesus' ancestors include a prostitute, an adulteress, a woman who committed incest, and a former pagan gentile?

> Christmas Card Theology ignores Jesus' ancestry. What does the Scripture say?
>
> Answer: Yes, Matthew 1:3, 5, 6. Jesus' ancestors include a prostitute (Tamar), an adulteress (Bathsheba), a woman who committed incest (Tamar), and a former pagan gentile (Ruth).
>
> Explanations:
>
> The prostitute who committed incest. Matthew 1:3, "and Judah fathered Perez and Zerah of Tamar." The story is in Genesis 38. One of Jesus' lineal ancestors, Judah son of Jacob, married the daughter of a gentile woman named Shua. She and he had three sons, Er, Onan, and Shelah. Judah arranged for Er to marry a woman named Tamar (whether gentile or Hebrew we do not know). Er was wicked, so the Lord killed him for his wickedness.
>
> Then, according to custom (a levirate marriage), Judah told Onan to "Go in to thy brother's wife, and marry her as her brother-in-law, and raise up seed to thy brother" (Genesis 38:8, LXX). But Onan knew the child would not be his heir, but his dead brother's heir, according to custom. So at the critical moment during sexual intercourse, Onan withdrew out of Tamar and ejaculated on the ground. That displeased the Lord, and the Lord killed Onan for his wickedness.
>
> Judah's third son Shelah, was too young to enter into a levirate marriage with Tamar. So Judah told Tamar to wait until Shelah was old enough and then he would give Shelah to Tamar to bear a son as an heir to her dead husband Er. She was to "remain a widow" in her father's house until Shelah was old enough. But, Judah broke his vow, fearing Shelah would die like Er and Onan.
>
> When Shelah grew older, Tamar understood Judah would not keep his vow. She pretended to be a prostitute, and Judah hired her services, but had no money with him to pay her. He promised her a goat. They had sexual intercourse. He then left to get the goat from the flock, but before he left she took his

"staff and cord" as pledges he would return with payment. While he was gone she left with the pledges.

Three months later Tamar was discovered to be pregnant. She was reported to Judah, who condemned her to be executed by burning. Tamar sent the pledges to him, and he admitted his guilt in withholding Shelah from her. Tamar bore twins, Perez and Zerah. Perez was a lineal ancestor of Jesus.

Tamar was not a prostitute, she played the part of a prostitute to gain a son as promised to her by her father-in-law Judah. Their sexual intercourse was incest because she was his daughter-in-law, Leviticus 18:15.

The adulteress. Matthew 1:6, "And David the king fathered Solomon of her of Uriah;" Luke 3:23, 31, "And Jesus himself was beginning about thirty years, being son ... of Nathan, of David."

The story is in 2 Samuel 11. At time when King David should have been out of the city defending Israel from its enemies—he sent his armies but he did not go with them—David saw from a distance a woman bathing on a roof top, Bathsheba, wife of Uriah. His lust was inflamed, he sent for her, he committed adultery with her. When Bathsheba became pregnant David had Uriah killed, and he took her as his wife. That child died. Then Bathsheba bore Solomon with David.

Solomon was not a lineal ancestor of Jesus. Matthew's gospel gives the royal lineage of Jesus as Messiah-King. We must turn to Luke 3:31 for the lineal ancestor of David to Jesus, which was David's son Nathan from Bathsheba, 1 Chronicles 3:5 (LXX), "And these were born to him in Jerusalem; Samaa, Sobab, Nathan, and Solomon; four of Bersabee the daughter of Amiel."

The Gentile. Matthew 1:5, 6, "and Boaz fathered Obed of Ruth; and Obed fathered Jesse; 6 and Jesse fathered David the king."

This story is told in the Book of Ruth.

During a time of famine in Bethlehem, during the times of the Judges, a man named Elimelech left Bethlehem with his wife,

Naomi, and his sons Mahlon and Chilion, to seek better conditions in Moab. The country of Moab was across the Jordan River at the south end of the east side of the Dead Sea.

During the course of time, Elimelech took Moabite wives, Orpah and Ruth, for his sons. They all lived in Moab for about ten years. Then Elimelech died, Mahlon died, and Chilion died. Naomi heard her former neighbors in Bethlehem were doing well and decided to return to Bethlehem. Ruth decided to go with her. Ruth made that famous declaration of faith, Ruth 1:16–17 (LXX).

> Intreat me not to leave thee, or to return from following thee; for whithersoever thou goest, I will go, and wheresoever thou lodgest, I will lodge; thy people shall be my people, and thy God my God. And wherever thou diest, I will die, and there will I be buried: the Lord do so to me, and more also, if I leave thee, for death only shall divide between me and thee

Naomi and Ruth returned to Bethlehem, found a place to live, and Ruth began gleaning in the fields for their food. Now Naomi did not tell Ruth that Naomi had a kinsmen in Bethlehem, who was also Ruth's kinsmen by her marriage to one of Naomi's sons. The kinsman's name was Boaz. Ruth went to glean in the fields, "and she happened by chance to come on a portion of the land of Booz, of the kindred of Elimelech," Ruth 2:3 (LXX).

Of course, nothing with the Lord is by chance. Over time, Boaz developed an interest in Ruth, that she might be his wife, and Ruth developed an interest in Boaz, that he might be her husband. There were some legal and inheritance issues to work out, but in the end Boaz married Ruth, and Boaz fathered Obed of Ruth; and Obed fathered Jesse; and Jesse fathered David the king, of whom was born Nathan, a lineal descendant of Jesus.

For all the details of Ruth and Boaz see my book, *A Private Commentary on the Bible: Ruth*.

54. What words of Joseph are recorded in the Christmas story?

> Christmas Card Theology does not include any words by or from Joseph. What does the Scripture say?
>
> Answer: The Scripture does not record any words by or from Joseph.
>
> Explanation: The Scripture gives a summary of Joseph's thoughts at Matthew 1:19–20. "But Joseph her husband, being righteous, and not willing to expose her publicly, desired to secretly divorce her. 20 But these things he having thought (his spirit was agitated), behold, a messenger of the Lord in a dream appeared to him, saying, 'Joseph, son of David, do not fear to receive Mariam as your wife, for that conceived in her is from the Holy Spirit.'"
>
> In every place where Joseph is mentioned (Matthew 1, 2; Luke 2) the Scripture does not give an account of any words spoken by or from Joseph.

55. Were the angels chubby little cherubs?

Christmas Card Theology uses several diverse depictions of angels, including chubby little cherubs. What does the Scripture say?

Answer: No.

Explanation: Luke 2:8–1, "And shepherds were in the same region, living in the fields and keeping watch by night over their flock. 9 And a messenger of the Lord stood by them, and the glory of the Lord shone around them, and they greatly feared. 10 And the messenger said to them, 'Do not fear. For behold, I proclaim to you good news, great joy, which will be to all the people. 11 For has been born to you today a savior who is Christ Lord, in David's city. 12 And this to you the sign: you will find a baby, swaddled, and lying in a barn.' 13 And at once there came with the messenger a multitude of the heavenly host, praising God and saying, 14 'Glory in the highest to God, and on earth peace among men of good will.'"

God's messengers, the *ággelos*, aka: "angels," are a race of spirit beings God created to be suitable for life in the spirit domain, just as humankind is a race of material beings God created to be suitable for life in the material domain.

The spirit beings do not have gender as humankind knows gender, and do not reproduce, Luke 20:34–36. Each messenger is an individual creation, each created to be suitable to the function for which they were created. Therefore, because not reproducing, and because individually created, there is no one common form possessed by all of God's messengers.

God's messengers cannot be said to have a material physical form because they are immaterial spirit beings. Yet they have some kind of defined form, because they are finite beings. As finite beings they are defined by time and space: in one place at any one moment in time. A "body" as a finite form suited for life in the immaterial spirit domain seems a suitable term.

The Scripture presents God's messengers in two kinds of "bodies." One kind of body is human in appearance. For example, Daniel 9:21; 11:5. Those messengers do not have wings. Other messengers are said to have many wings and many eyes. Those are the cherubim-seraphim.

Isaiah 6:1–3 (LXX), "And it came to pass in the year in which king Ozias died, that I saw the Lord sitting on a high and exalted throne, and the house was full of his glory. And seraphs stood round about him: each one had six wings: and with two they covered their face, and with two they covered their feet, and with two they flew. And one cried to the other, and they said, 'Holy, holy, holy is the Lord of hosts: the whole earth is full of his glory.'"

The word "seraph" means "burner." Isaiah is describing the bright appearance of the cherubim around the throne.

Ezekiel 10 describes cherubim with wings around a vision of God's throne. Ezekiel 10:20–22 (LXX), "This is the living creature which I saw under the God of Israel by the river of Chobar; and I knew that they were cherubs. Each one had four faces, and each one had eight wings; and under their wings was the likeness of men's hands. And as for the likeness of their faces, these are the same faces which I saw under the glory of the God of Israel by the river of Chobar: and they went each straight forward."

The Book of Revelation describes cherubs around God's throne. Revelation 4:5–8, "And in the midst of the throne and encircling the throne four living creatures, full of eyes front and back. 7 And the first living creature like a lion, and the second living creature like a calf, and the third living creature having the face as of a human being, and the fourth living creature as an eagle flying. 8 And the four living creatures, they one for one each had six wings encircling and within full of eyes. And they do not have rest day and night, saying, 'Holy, holy, holy the Lord God Almighty, the one having been, and the one being, and the one coming.'"

Lucifer (who rebelled and became Satan) is also described as a cherub, Ezekiel 28:14.

The messengers in Luke 2:8–14 were not cherubim. They were not flying.

56. Did Jesus' family celebrate his birthday as we do today?

> Christmas Card Theology teaches nothing about birthday celebrations. What does the Scripture say?
>
> Answer: The Scripture does not say.
>
> Explanation: Jesus and his family celebrated the three mandatory Jewish Feasts (Unleavened Bread, Pentecost, Tabernacles), and Jesus probably celebrated Hanukkah (the Feast of Dedication) because he was in the temple at that feast, John 10:2.
>
> Scripture does not require Christians to celebrate any annual feasts or birthdays. Not Jesus' birth, not Easter, not any annual celebrations. Such celebrations are traditions developed during the history of the New Testament church. That does not mean such celebrations are wrong, but one should always bear in mind that traditions, of any kind, are wonderful servants but terrible masters.

57. Were sheep, cattle, a donkey, kings, angels, shepherds, and a little drummer boy present in the stable after Jesus was born?

> Christmas Card Theology teaches all sorts of people and animals were present to celebrate Jesus' birth in the barn at the Tower of the Flock. What does the Scripture say?
>
> Answer: No.
>
> Explanation: The only people present in the barn at the Tower of the Flock after Jesus was born were Joseph, Mariam, Jesus, and an unknown number of shepherds.
>
> The donkey that pulled the cart with the family's possessions (see Question 18) may have been in the barn. There were no sheep in the barn because the sheep were with the shepherds who were "living in the fields and keeping watch by night over their flock," Luke 2:8.
>
> The Hebrews did not keep cattle, the angels never visited the barn, the only king in the region was Herod, and no one told him Jesus was born, and little boys of the times did not have toy drums and were where they were supposed to be, in bed at home.
>
> I once saw a photograph of a Nativity scene with sheep, cattle, a donkey, kings, angels, shepherds, a little drummer boy, and a figure of Yoda from the Star Wars movies. The likelihood of sheep, cattle, kings, angels, and drummer boys in the barn after Jesus' birth is the same as the presence of Yoda, a fictional character.
>
> Christmas Card Theology is not the Christmas story.

Sources and Resources

Aharoni, Yohanan, and Michael Avi-Yohan. *The MacMillan Bible Atlas*. Rev. New York, NY: 1968.

Borowski, Oded. *Agriculture in Iron Age Israel*. Atlanta, GA: American School of Oriental Research, 2002.

Brenton, Sir Lancelot, C. L. *The Septuagint with Apocrypha: English*. London: Samuel Bagster & Sons, 1851. Reprinted http://ecmarsh.com, 2010.

Bromiley, Geoffrey W. Gen. Ed. *The International Standard Bible Encyclopedia (ISBE)*. Revised 1982. Reprinted, Grand Rapids, MI: William B. Eerdmans Publishing Company, 1992.

Chill, Abraham. *The Mitzvot, the Commandments and Their Rationale*. Jerusalem: Keter Books, 1990.

Danby, Herbert. *The Mishnah*. Oxford, England: Oxford University Press, 1933.

Dreyer, F.C.H. and E. Weller. *Roman Catholicism in the Light of Scripture*. Chicago, IL: Moody Press, 1960.

Harris, R. Laird; Gleason L. Archer, Jr.; and Bruce K. Waltke. *Theological Wordbook of the Old Testament*. 2 vols. Chicago, IL: Moody Press, 1980.

Hollingsworth, David R. and James D. Quiggle. *Old and New Testament Chronology*. Amazon/KDP, 2015.

Quiggle, James D. *A Private Commentary on the Bible: John 1–12*. Amazon/KDP, 2014.

_____. *A Private Commentary on the Bible: Luke's Gospel 1:1–12:59*. Amazon/KDP, 2021.

_____. *A Private Commentary on the Bible: Mark's Gospel*. Amazon/KDP, 2016.

_____. *A Private Commentary on the Bible: Matthew's Gospel*. Amazon/KDP, 2016.

_____. *A Private Commentary on the Bible: Philippians*, Amazon/KDP, 2020.

_____. *Adam and Eve, A Biography and Theology*. Amazon/KDP, 2011.

_____. *Angelology, A True History of Angels.* Amazon/KDP, 2017, 2020.

_____. *James Quiggle Translation New Testament.* Amazon/KDP, 2023.

_____. *The Christmas Story as Told by God*, Amazon/KDP, 2019.

_____. *God Became Incarnate.* Amazon/KDP, 2014.

Ramsay, Sir William M. 1898. *Was Christ Born in Bethlehem?* 1898. Reprinted, Minneapolis, MN: James Family Publishing, 1978.

Roberts, Alexander and James Donaldson. *Ante-Nicene Fathers*, vol. 1, *The Apostolic Fathers, Justin Martyr, Irenaeus.* 1885, Reprinted, Peabody, MA: Hendrickson Publishers, 1995.

Schaff, Philip. *Nicene and Post–Nicene Fathers, First Series.* Vol. 3. *Augustin: On the Holy Trinity, Doctrinal Treatises, Moral Treatises.* 1887. Reprinted, Peabody, MA: Hendrickson Publishers, 1999.

Schaff, Philip and Henry Wace. *Nicene and Post-Nicene Fathers. Second Series.* Vol. 6. *Jerome: Letters and Select Works.* 1893. Reprinted, Peabody MA: Hendrickson Publishers, 1999.

Zodhiates, Spiros. *The Complete Word Study Dictionary: New Testament.* Revised. Chattanooga, TN: AMG Publishers, 1993.

www.ingramcontent.com/pod-product-compliance
Lightning Source LLC
Chambersburg PA
CBHW060828050426
42453CB00008B/626